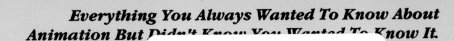

Everything You Always Wanted To Know About
Animation But Didn't Know You Wanted To Know It.

Cartoon
CONFIDENTIAL

JIM KORKIS
JOHN CAWLEY

Introduction by
BILL HANNA

Malibu Graphics, Inc.

CARTOON CONFIDENTIAL

Jim Korkis
John Cawley
Writers

•

Marc Hansen
Cover Illustration

Tom Smith
Cover Coloring

•

Dave Olbrich
Publisher

Kim Scholter
Publishing
Coordinator

Chris Ulm
Editor-in-Chief

Dan Danko
Editor

Mickie Villa
Art Director

Tom Mason
Creative Director

Acknowledgements

It's time to tip the hat to those who gave direct help by correcting or supplying information. There's also the indirect help from the team of writers and historians who have strived to make animation history a somewhat accurate field.

A big thank you goes to "Mr. Animation" himself, film historian Mark Kausler for help in describing some of the more obscure animated Oscar winning cartoons. Other names include: Joe Adamson, Sarah Baisley, Joe Barbera, Mike Barrier, Jerry Beck, Mike Cadlec, Leslie Carbaga, Bob Clampett, Karl Cohen, John Culhane, Harvey Deneroff, Will Friedwald, Denis Gifford, Gary Grossman, Bill Hanna, Jack Hannah, Chuck Jones, Jeff Lenburg, Harry McCracken, Leonard Maltin, Bob Miller, Dave Mruz, Fred Patten, Steve Rowe, Bill Scott, David R. Smith and George S. Woolery and sadly some people we've most likely forgotten but who will kill us when they don't see their names.

This Book Is Dedicated To Our Parents
John and Barbara Korkis
John and Kathryn Cawley

Other Books By The Authors
by Jim Korkis & John Cawley
The Encyclopedia of Cartoon Superstars (Pioneer Books)
How To Create Animation (Pioneer Books)

by John Cawley
The Films of Don Bluth (Image)
Who's Who Of Animation (Get Animated)

by Jim Korkis
Hooked!
The Complete History Of Peter Pan And Captain Hook (Image)

CARTOON CONFIDENTIAL
Published by Malibu Graphics Publishing Group
5321 Sterling Center Dr.
Westlake Village, CA 91361
818/889-9800.
Printed in the USA. First Printing.
ISBN# 1-56398-005-3 $14.95 • $17.95 In Canada

-TABLE OF CONTENTS-

It's Not Confidential Anymore!

Rumors. Gossip. Secrets.

Over the years, we've heard more than our share of stories. In fact, animation is a storytelling medium with a host of interesting characters both on and off screen. So, it is not surprising that some stories have been forgotten, exaggerated, or twisted out of shape.

This book is an attempt to finally get into print the true facts before they are lost forever. Included are those interesting tidbits only known to a chosen few as well as those items that will hopefully jog a fond memory or two.

You don't need to start with the first chapter. Jump to a topic that looks interesting and dive in. Each chapter is a self-contained unit ready to take you into the World of Toons.

For those who wonder how two people can write one book, it's very simple. One of us writes the first draft of a chapter and the second one re-writes and corrects the first. Then the first one grumbles that all the best stuff has been changed and we argue and discuss and explain and justify and finally come up with something we both can live with when it is in print. It's quite civilized.

Preliminary drafts for some of these chapters have appeared as magazine articles elsewhere during the last few years in an attempt to find corrections and additions. We found so much new and improved information that we couldn't include it all. Hopefully we've chosen the best pieces to share with you.

Have fun!
Jim Korkis
John Cawley

A Word About Errors

"oops "

Though every effort is made to be correct and catch typing and typesetting errors, some always slip through and all authors cringe when they find them. If you have any corrections or additions, simply write to us at Post Office Box 1458, Burbank, California 91507. An SASE (self-addressed-stamped-envelope) will guarantee some kind of reply.

Copyrights

All characters pictured are copyrighted their respective owners and are individually acknowledged in each chapter. The authors have attempted to correctly identify the appropriate copyright holders but since the world of animation is a particularly tangled and ever changing web of connections, we wish to apologize if any misidentification has occurred and will make the appropriate changes in future editions if we are notified.

Foreword by William Hanna

Of all the material I have ever read on the subject of animated cartoons, *Cartoon Confidential* is by far the most comprehensive coverage of this particular art form.

April of this year will mark my sixtieth year of continuous involvement in this wonderful crazy cartoon business. *Cartoon Confidential* has covered every exciting change that has occurred in our industry during my lifetime, from early Mickey Mouse to the present craze of collecting animation art. It has all been covered, and covered very well, like with a blanket of beautiful orchids.

Don't miss John and Jim's great new efforts.
Bill Hanna
March, 1991

Bill Hanna is half of the famous Hanna-Barbera team. With Joe Barbera, he has directed more Oscar-winning shorts than any other animation director. The Emmy-winning team is responsible for creating such Cartoon Superstars as Tom and Jerry, Huckleberry Hound, the Flintstones and Yogi Bear, as well as bringing life to the Jetsons, Quick Draw McGraw, Johnny Quest, Magilla Gorilla, Scooby Doo, Snagglepuss, the Smurfs and scores of other animated favorites.

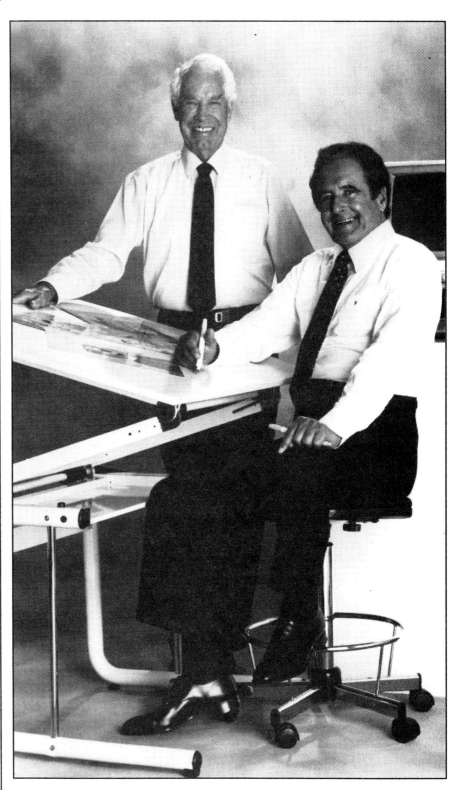

Bill Hanna (standing) with long time partner *Joe Barbera* in a photo celebrating their 50th anniversary working together, 1989

TOP SECRET

CHAPTER ONE:

EVERYTHING YOU WANTED TO KNOW ABOUT ANIMATION, BUT DIDN'T KNOW YOU WANTED TO KNOW IT

"What makes it move? "

"Who thinks all that stuff up?"

"Why can't they make cartoons like they used to? "

"Does a computer do all that?"

These are typical questions from those who give a casual notice to the world of animation, such as film critics and mass media

it with antiquated terms, modern buzz words or simple ignorance. It matters not the subject. Comic art aficionados cringe when "funny book" is mentioned as much as science fiction buffs ruffle at the use of "sci-fi." This can even apply to locations—try saying "Frisco" in San Francisco some time and you may end

general, mass media—with mixed results. These crusading TV journalists and critics will pick up these key terms and try to twist them into a simplified explanation for the point they are trying to make. This often happens at the expense of accuracy and historical truth.

For those who want just some simple answers to the complex topics of animation, here is a guide structured to teach anyone interested in animation all they need to know to discuss the subject and show up the buzz-word bullies. To make it even easier, the guide is broken down by the topics specific questions raise !

What Makes It Move?

What is animation? This sounds like a simple enough question and for most people there is a simple answer. Cartoons. Cartoons with funny characters that move, and talk (not a prerequisite) and make us believe they are more than just lines on paper.

Officially, animated characters don't move. That statement seems pretty obvious, but even today people are uncertain as to how hundreds of drawings can appear to have life. To them, it seems that there must be some complicated technical mumbo-jumbo that can explain such an odd experience.

There is. It is called "persistence of vision."

authors. To these questions, good answers would be, "What is *it*? " "What *stuff*? " "By *cartoons* do you mean theatrical shorts? features? funny ones? or what?" Finally, "A computer only does what it's told to."

Nothing is probably more irritating to anyone who enjoys a topic and studies it than the destruction and confusion caused by those who discuss

Above: UPA's stylized designs did not always mean limited animation. (Still from Magoo Makes News, *1955) ©1991 UPA*

up leaving more than your heart in that city.

To find simple information on animation, the average person is generally at the mercy of scholarly text books who treat cartoons and animation as some form of classical art or science. Authors of such volumes toss unfamiliar terms around that are used in the business. Many of these terms find their way into the

When a single picture is flashed at the eye, the brain retains that image longer than it is actually registered on the retina. When a movie projector flashes a series of pictures in rapid order (especially with the images only slightly changed) the effect is one of continuous motion. The brain remembers the previous picture when it is seeing the next picture.

Persistence of vision is what makes all movies work. Today, films are projected at a standard 24 frames (images) per second. In the days of silent movies, film speed ranged from 16 to 60, depending on the (hand) cranking and producer. This variable speed is what makes many old films "flicker" when run on today's projectors. With the coming of sound, the speed was standardized.

Unlike films, though, animation is not merely recording in real time what was seen by the camera man. In animation, each frame is shot separately. Anything can be made to move when using the motion picture camera frame by frame: drawings, puppets, rocks, even stationary people. This gives animation the advantage of being able to create its own universe and rules. It also increases the cost since it can take several days to photograph (shoot) a mere minute of screen time. (And this does not take into

account the work done previously to allow the filming, such as drawing or sculpting.)

All cartoons are animated but all animation is *not* cartoons

The terms "cartoons" and "animation" are not always equal and interchangeable. Saying "animation" is like saying "TV." There are many kinds of TV and many ways of dividing TV into smaller categories ("live," "sitcoms," "documentary," etc.) The same is true with animation. In fact, since some names to describe animation are the property of specific businesses, it can be illegal to use them loosely! (Not all photocopies are Xeroxes nor

are all gelatin desserts Jell-O.)

When discussing animated shorts, features, TV shows and videos, the more specific you get will not only make communication easier, but will show you have more intelligence than the average media meddler and film critic. All of the following terms can be easily covered by the word "animation."

Cel Animation

This is the most common form of animation and in fact when the general public talks about animation, this is the type that they usually have in mind. Films using this method start with someone drawing an image (hence "cartoon" since it was like newspaper comics/

Below:
The Man From Button Willow, a cel animated feature film from 1964, starred an animated caricature of actor Dale Robertson. Robertson voiced the character as well as financed much of the film. ©1964. United Screen Arts

cartoons). Sometimes referred to as "drawn animation," cel animation comes from the term celluloid, the chemical substance of the early plastic sheets which were drawn upon (or traced upon) and placed over the background and shot (and now worth mucho dinero). Acetate is used today but as with many things, the old name stuck and today the transparent sheets are still called "cels" (one "l" please).

Cel animation is used for both full animation, where everything moves, and limited animation, where only parts move. As this century nears its end, more and more studios using cel

Opposite page: The clay animated California Raisins. ©1991 Will Vinton Productions

Below: Yogi Bear's tie and collar helped Hanna-Barbera hide the fact that his head was on a different cel than his body. © 1988 Worldvision Enterprises, Inc.

animation are eliminating the cels by coloring the drawings on computers and transferring this directly to film. Even Disney features like *The Rescuers Down Under* did not use cels in the production. However, since the visual effect is the same, this term will probably remain for years to come.

Clay Animation
Instead of using drawings (like cel animation), some artists and studios use clay mixtures and synthetic substitutes like Plasticine to create a three dimensional image. (Real clay can dry out under hot studio lights resulting in things breaking apart.) Clay animation is especially good

at showing metamorphosis as it "melts" from one form to another. Clay figures can actually be quite large so that more detail can be added and movement can be done more easily.

Though clay animation has been around for decades, for most of its life, it was relegated to independent or festival films. The only popular clay animation was found in the Gumby and Pokey films created by Art Clokey in the Fifties. In the late Eighties all of that changed. Thanks to the popularity of the commercials with the California Raisins, music videos by such top names as Peter Gabriel, and segments seen on *Pee Wee's Playhouse*, clay animation came into its own.

Considered the "king of clay" is Will Vinton, whose trademarked "Claymation" has brought life to the California Raisins, Domino's Noid and others. Only Vinton uses the term "Claymation," having trademarked it. Other producers and artists are doing "clay animation." Thanks to the pioneering and successful work of animators like Vinton and Jimmy Picker (*Sundae In New York*), clay animation is receiving greater recognition.

Puppet Animation
Although not very popular here in America, puppet animation is recognized and encouraged

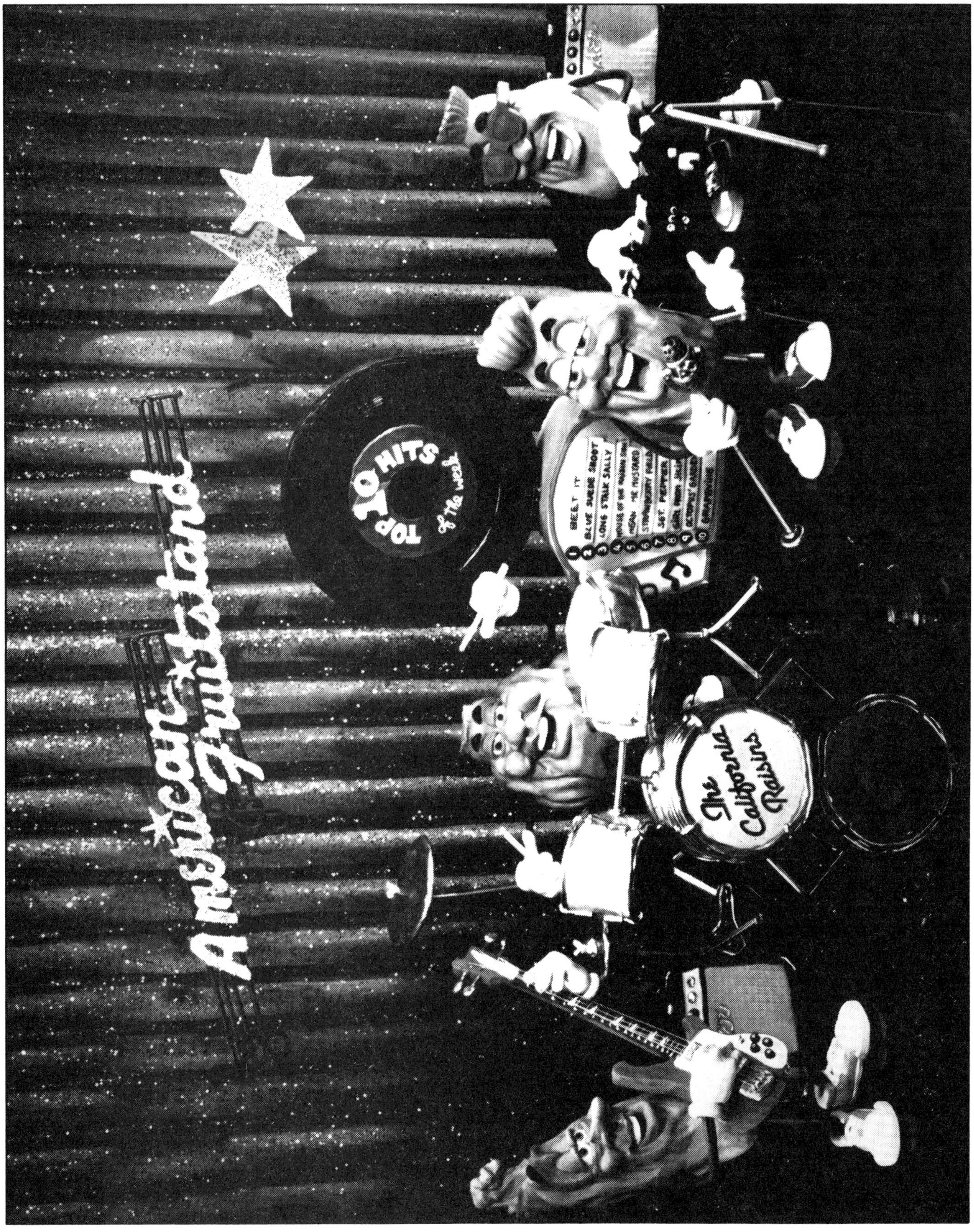
American Bandstand
TOP 10 HITS of the week
The California Raisins

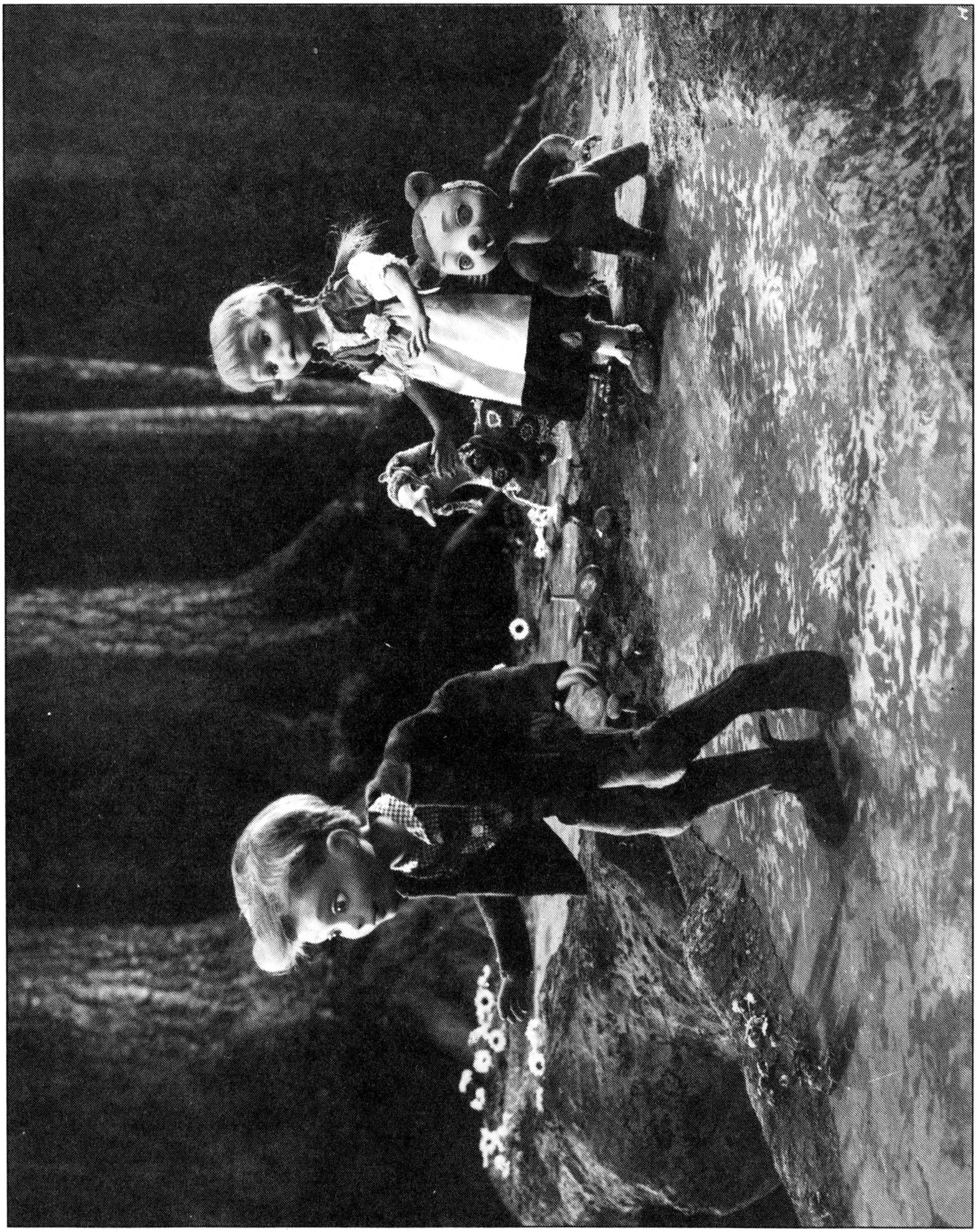

in Europe and the East. Most of the leading puppet animators have come from abroad and one of them, George Pal, achieved recognition here via his Puppetoons shorts of the 1930s and 40s. Puppet figures are able to stand on their own and support their own weight. Most puppets have an armature of wood, metal or wire. This armature is a skeleton that allows the puppet to move slightly at body joints like elbows and knees and maintain that position. Like clay animation, puppet animation allows three dimensional backgrounds. With appropriate lighting a very dramatic effect can be achieved.

At the video store one can find many examples of puppet animation. The most familiar to U.S. audiences would probably be the perennial Christmas special favorite, *Rudolph The Red-Nosed Reindeer*. Produced by Rankin-Bass (with the work being done in other countries), *Rudolph* was the first of several Rankin-Bass specials using puppet animation. They even produced *Mad Monster Party*, a full length feature with puppet caricatures of such stars as Boris Karloff and Phyllis Diller. Other features showcasing puppet animation include *Hansel And Gretel* (1959) and *Pinchcliffe Grandprix* (1981)

Stop Motion Animation

A sub-category of puppet animation would be what most people refer to as "stop motion" animation. (Actually all animation is created this way, i.e. via "stop motion" photography.) Creators like Willis O'Brien and Ray Harryhausen are legendary filmmakers in this area. Their figures in such classics as *King Kong* (the original) and *The 7th Voyage Of Sinbad* are designed and operated in the same manner as puppet animation. Harryhausen even attempted to rename his process as "Dynamation" (and later to "Dynarama" when doing wide screen films), but it is still generally called "stop motion." By placing the

Opposite page: Hansel and Gretel was a puppet animated feature film released in the U.S. in 1954. ©1954 Michael Myerberg Productions

Below: Special effect creatures, such as these skeletons from Ray Harryhausen's Jason And The Argonauts, are created using stop motion animation. ©1963 Columbia Pictures

puppet in front of a movie screen and re-shooting the movie (frame by frame) with the puppet, the final film gives the impression that the puppet is interacting with the live actors.

Silhouette Animation

One of the least common today, silhouette animation was once fairly popular in Europe and the East. This is a process where paper cut-outs are placed between the camera and a light source (like a light board). Only the shadows are photographed. An animation pioneer who used this process was German born Lotte Reiniger, who in 1926 completed *The Adventures Of Prince Achmed* (one of the first animated feature films). She later

moved to Canada where she continued making silhouette films (including a sound and color re-make of *Achmed*) up to her death in the 1980s.

George Lucas produced an animated feature in the early Eighties with John Korty in a similar process that they called "Lumage." Using the shadow process along with a multiplane style camera (allowing layers of the film to move independently of each other) gave tremendous depth to the final film. The movie, *Twice Upon A Time*, received almost no theatrical screenings, but was released on home video in the early Nineties.

Computer Animation

There are still many people unclear on this newest form of animation. They are under the mistaken belief that somehow, miraculously, the computer is able to draw and move objects. In computer animation, a human is still needed. It is the programmer or artist who inputs information into the computer through a variety of methods. Similar to clay and puppet animation, computers are still largely used for short independent films (the Oscar winning *Tin Toy*), as special effects (*Tron*) or in TV commercials.

Where the computer saves time and money is the fact that it can rotate the object, rotate the point of view and given the proper

Right: Computer generated drawing for the villain Blastarr from the Captain Power And The Soldiers Of The Future *TV series, a live action series utilizing computer generated villains. ©1987 Arcca Animation, Inc.*

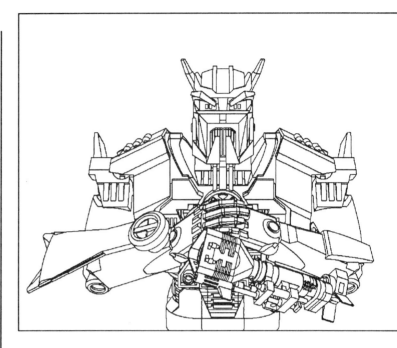

information it can have the object move or float. This has made it popular for commercials and corporate logos. In feature animation production, the computer has been especially useful in the creation of mechanical effects such as the clockwork interior in Disney's *The Great Mouse Detective* (now called *The Adventures Of The Great Mouse Detective*) and the crashing car in Don Bluth's *All Dogs Go To Heaven*.

Also being used in some production is the computer as an inbetweener. Since all animators only produce the "key" drawings of movement, perhaps one or two per second, whereas as many as 24 might be needed, other artists (called "assistants" or "in betweeners") will do the rest. Some studios are now using computers to do the drawings "in between" the

keys.

Is it half-full or half-limited?

Sure to come up in animated conversations are the two key terms in the art: full and limited. These are probably the most misused and misunderstood terms, even by animators. As if the definitions weren't fuzzy enough, because of the publicity blitz surrounding *Who Framed Roger Rabbit* the general media became aware of "shooting on ones." As one movie critic team stated, this made *Who Framed Roger Rabbit* better than Snow White because the earlier Disney classic had been "shot on twos." The difference being that shooting on "ones" means that each drawing is shot only once, so there are 24 pieces of art in every second. Shooting on twos means each drawing is shot twice, making 12 pieces of art in every 24 frames.

Full Animation

Whenever Disney, Don Bluth or Steven Spielberg come out with a new feature, the term " full animation" comes up. Critics and the media are quick to pick up on this buzz word. For some, it means a lushness of animation and color where everything moves all the time. (This definition also can mean that the subject is "overanimated.") Others use the term when they are really referring to "character animation" and talking about animated characters that have achieved a sense of reality apart from the screen. Still others use the term to define what good animation is and bad animation isn't.

Generally, full animation does suggest more drawings (though not necessarily good drawings), that each character moves individually and that all of the character moves. However, full animation should never be confused with "good" animation. Full animation can be dull and awkward when not done properly, or not backed up with proper story or direction. It can also be the stuff that dreams are made of.

Despite the publicity, most of the classic "full animation" from the old days of "classic animation" was actually shot on twos. Shooting on twos (or many times just "shooting twos") creates the illusion of smooth movement. Unless there is some reason why a film or a sequence needs to be "shot on ones," most animators working on full animation will usually do their work "shooting twos or threes." (*Roger Rabbit* required "ones" due to the need to match the characters to live action footage shot from a continually moving camera.)

For the general audience, the final animated film will look the same whether shot on ones or twos. In fact, if poorly directed or shot, ones can look more static than twos. However shooting on "eights" (eight frames for each drawing) or "twelves" such is usually done on Saturday morning is noticeable. (See "Limited Animation" below.)

Limited Animation

Limited animation refers to the fact that less drawings are being used per second and less movement is taking place.

Generally, this is thought of as a cheap form of animation. Supposedly, all limited animation is bad animation. This is simply not the case. Both the Disney studio and the artists at UPA made effective use of limited animation. However, limited animation is much more noticeable when the idea, the story and the characters are also limited in inspiration and imagination.

The UPA studio, which starred such characters as Mr. Magoo and Gerald McBoing Boing, felt that strong design and story were more important than recreating movement. In fact, UPA was formed by many former Disney animators who felt restricted by Disney's desire to make animation more and more realistic. Often the animation in these shorts is as "full" as a Disney film in number of drawings. It's just the movement is not as fluid by design.

A bigger leap into limited animation occurred in the Fifties when studios began making cartoons for TV. Some of the early series, like *Crusader Rabbit* featured almost no animation. They used camera movements and slight animation to tell stories. Today, this scan and dissolve process is sometimes called "animatics."

Hanna-Barbera became the kings of limited animation when they started their studio in the late Fifties. The Oscar winning directors of dozens of Tom and Jerry cartoons found that TV budgets didn't allow for the lush animation they were used to. They devised, what they liked to call, "planned animation." By carefully planning the movements and drawings, less drawing time, and thus less money, was needed.

This was accomplished by dividing the body into parts so only the parts moving needed to be animated. A body would be drawn once. Then the animator would only draw the two legs walking, or a hand waving, or a head turning. In the beginning this was often obvious as the color of the character's head, or hand, or feet would change when they would move. To make the effect a bit less noticeable, Hanna-Barbera designed most of their characters to wear ties so that the head would not rest directly on the

Below: Don Bluth's Dragon's Lair video game animation featured full animation. ©1983 Don Bluth

shoulders.

Limited animation can indeed be terrible but it has been shown many times that limited animation does not prevent the creation of memorable characters and interesting stories. There are many cartoons from the Thirties and Forties which were animated in full animation and are deadly dull today. Despite the illusion of movement, they are tough sitting through even for historical purposes. On the other hand, one of the

most limited animation series has achieved cult status and the characters are instantly recognized and loved by a large part of the American population. The adventures of Rocky and Bullwinkle and their friends were some of the most carelessly animated episodes of all time. Because of money restrictions (most of the animation was being done in Mexico) the quality of individual episodes vary widely with animation not matching, mouths not

moving at the appropriate time and a host of other elementary flaws. Yet a retrospective of Jay Ward cartoons can pull in a sell-out crowd while a retrospective of classic Van Beuren shorts of the Thirties would play to an almost empty house.

As the popularity of *The Simpsons* shows, audiences are as entertained by strong characters, strong scripts and good direction as good animation. It's nice when all elements are present, but past performance shows that if any element of an animated film needs to be weak, audiences will accept weak animation over almost any other aspect.

Who Does All That Stuff?

The person, or persons, responsible for any animated film depends on what kind of production it is. Animation can most easily be broken down into two categories by simply asking, "who's the boss?" This helps distinguish between the two main forces in animation (and most film making) today: The Studio and The Independent. Sadly, few discussions on animation ever care to make that distinction. Comparing a studio product, such as *The Smurfs* or *An American Tail* to an independent film is unfair. Not only are the budgets greatly different, but so are the intents.

The Studio

Almost all of the animation seen by the general public is produced by a major studio. Feature films, TV series, specials and most TV commercials are all produced by a studio. The studio is in what is called the "business of entertainment." Whether the studio is Disney, which employs hundreds of artists in its studio, or Hanna-Barbera, who uses artists located around the world, studio animation is driven by one force: profits.

Though "artists" may scoff at such a drive, it is this simple motivation that has created most of the world's best loved animation. If Disney had not wanted more profits, he would not have turned to sound, and then to color and finally produced *Snow White* and the subsequent Disney classic features. While it is often stated that animation (and film) are an art form, it must not be forgotten they are also a form of entertainment. Only the most zealous artist (and some "well meaning" social directors who continue to insist upon blandness or education in all media) would have animation without entertainment.

In fact, like general motion pictures and television, the profits (or ratings in TV) are one of the best ways to judge the success of a production. It can be argued that the general public is not well enough equipped to make such important judgments, but it is one way to rate material. Often can be heard the cry that what people really want is quality entertainment. Article after article complain about current animation and state that if it went back to the classic style audiences would beat a path to its door. Time and again, this statement has been proved as incorrect as correct. As every producer would say, it is almost impossible to tell what will attract an audience.

The Independent

Independent producers are those who strive to stretch the field of animation. It is their films that make the rounds in small festivals and show up occasionally in retrospectives. These are the films that win festival awards (and frequently the Oscar for best animated short). They come in a variety of lengths, subjects and media. However, they all have one thing in common. They are one artist's vision and experimentation.

These films are far more common outside the U.S. In Europe, Canada, and other countries, governments offer grants and financial support to encourage artists in film making. In the U.S., most of the independent films come via the student filmmaker or studio artist who saves his own money to produce projects on the side.

Many of these films are well done and thoughtful.

Everything You Wanted To Know About Animation...

They are also often tedious and self indulgent. Since the filmmaker need only please himself, that is sometimes his only appreciative audience. But, as in all experimentation, there are often flashes of brilliance that will carry over into the other sector of animation (studios) ever expanding the art form on all levels.

In fact, many studios actually encourage independent efforts. Much of the experimental computer

Below: Even Disney's Pinocchio seems confused by the animation process. © Walt Disney Productions

films currently being produced are done so with a studio's blessing. The studios hope the experiments will create even more uses for the computer by increasing its potential.

An Animation Know-It-All

If you've made it this far, you now have the basic knowledge and terms needed to discuss animation in a competent way. In fact, you have more information than most film critics and media writers. Now comes

the hard part, putting up with all those who have read an article in a newspaper or seen a two-minute segment on a TV program and feel they know everything. Don't be too hard on such individuals. That over animated, under informed person may be in the business...and if there is one certainty about the art form, there are many in it who are just "full of" animation information, limited as it may be.

©W.D.P.

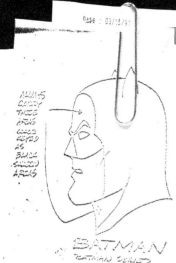

ALWAYS
CARRY
THESE
AREAS
COLOR
KEYED
AS
BLACK
SHADOW
AREAS

BATMAN
BATMAN SERIES

TOP SEC-RET

CHAPTER TWO:

THE ANIMATED SUPER-HEROES OF THE '60S

The Animated Superheroes Of The Sixties

In the Sixties, superhero comic books were receiving considerable attention thanks in part to the publicity surrounding the live-action *Batman* show and Marvel Comics catching the attention of college students. For a short three year period during this time, Saturday morning television left the

Joe Barbera (left) and Bill Hanna in a publicity photo promoting the prime time special The World Of Secret Squirrel And Atom Ant. ©1965 Hanna Barbera

funny animal barnyard and faster than a speeding bullet, superheroes filled that special morning with violent adventures and horrible monsters.

Back in 1965, network TV on Saturday morning still consisted mostly of theatrical repeats (*Heckle & Jeckle, Tom & Jerry, Porky Pig*, etc.) and

re-runs of prime time shows (*The Jetsons, Top Cat*, etc.). No serious animated super characters flew across the Saturday morning television screen. There were no mysterious dual identity crusaders who fought for truth, justice and the American way. In 1965, the best viewers could enjoy were animal parodies of the superhero genre. The new *Atom Ant/Secret Squirrel* show introduced a new super creature to join such super animal staples as Mighty Mouse and Underdog. The next year, all of that would change and a host of amazing human characters would be unleashed upon an eager audience.

In the Fall of 1966, Saturday morning took a different direction and it set into motion a series of events that would forever alter animation. The change is often credited to the then head of CBS daytime programming, Fred Silverman. It was he who felt that children, who read comics, would be more attracted to shows that emulated that medium. He also felt that the time period would be better served with new programming rather than repeats. Under his direction, CBS dropped almost every series of the previous season and replaced it with superhero shows.

Though it may be easy to

state that Silverman/CBS were ahead of their time, they just barely beat the other networks: both ABC and NBC debuted adventure and more comic book-based programming in minor amounts that Fall. In fact, over one-third of all shows on Saturday morning in the Fall of 1966 were adventure/comic based.

Perhaps the biggest influence was the introduction of *The New Adventures Of Superman*. The series brought a comic legend to Saturday morning as well as built one of the major early SatAM studios. It was the first television series of the (then) young Filmation studio. At the time, Filmation had only been in business about three years with most of its time devoted to producing commercials and to developing an animated sequel to *The Wizard Of Oz*. When Silverman obtained the rights to the Superman character, he decided the then-struggling Filmation would bring a different look to the series.

Filmation took great care to insure that their first series would be an accurate reflection of the then-current Superman comic books, just as the Fleischer series of Superman cartoons in the Forties mirrored the Joe Shuster-Jerry Siegel stories that had been appearing at that time. Filmation hired Mort Weisinger as story

Filmation's Superman and Krypto. ©1991 DC Comics, Inc.

consultant. Weisinger was one of the most important influences in the comic book career of Superman.

Weisinger, a pulp writer and editor, joined National Comics in 1940 and started his 30 year career as editor of the Superman family of magazines. It was under Weisinger's editorship that many of the aspects of the Superman legend were created such as Kryptonite, the many survivors of Krypton, the Phantom Zone, Krypto the Superdog and Supergirl. Weisinger had also assisted on the Superman serials and the television series.

Scripting chores were turned over to some top DC writers including Arnold Drake ("The Many Faces of Dr. Nucleus"), Bob Haney ("Can A Luthor Change His Spots"), William Finger ("Lava Men"), William Woolfolk ("The Abominable

Iceman"), George Kashdan ("The Two Faces of Superman") and Leo Dorfman ("The Gorilla Gang"). Each episode contained two Superman cartoons and one Superboy cartoon.

Many of the Filmation cartoons were based on comic book stories. For example, the episode "Superboy-Devil of a Time" was an adaptation of "Superman's Black Magic" (Superman 138, July 1960) and "Superboy-The Super Clown of Smallville" was taken from "The Super Clown of Metropolis" (Superman 136, April 1960).

To help maintain the

Sixties model sheet of Filmation's Batman. ©1991 DC Comics, Inc.

proper tone, Filmation also hired Bud Collyer to do the voice of Clark "Superman" Kent. Collyer had voiced the Man of Steel in the popular radio series of the Forties, as well as the Fleischer animated cartoons. Also in that radio series were Joan Alexander as Lois Lane and Jackson Beck as the narrator and incidental voices . Both of these fine performers were also hired by Filmation to recreate their roles. (These old veterans may have had some input into the scripting since the cartoon series also featured a Daily Planet copy boy named Beanie, who was a character on the radio show.)

The New Adventures Of Superman was a huge success, bringing in ratings previously unnoticed for Saturday morning programming. Perhaps its success was the result of the uniqueness of being totally new animation and being serious. (Those same reasons are cited for the smash success of *He-Man And The Masters Of The Universe,* which began the syndication animation boom of the 1980s.) Or perhaps it was the result of being so faithful to the original, popular character who already had a high recognition factor.

Helping *Superman* on CBS were a number of great

series, but only one was based on a previously known character: *The Lone Ranger*. This version of the masked rider of the plains had science fictional elements similar to the live action show *The Wild Wild West*. The animated series even had a counterpart to *WWW*'s Dr. Miguelito Loveless; the Lone Ranger battled Tiny Tom in several episodes.

Trying to save licensing fees CBS also had shows that featured new creations such as *Frankenstein Jr. And The Impossibles*, *Space Ghost* and *The Mighty Heroes*. Frankenstein Jr. was a huge robot controlled by Buzz Conroy, a young boy whose father was a famous scientist. The Impossibles were a rock group who doubled as superheroes. Both are largely forgotten today. But the other two series have developed strong cult followings.

Space Ghost, from Hanna-Barbera, was definitely one of the most popular super characters from this time period. Space Ghost patrolled outer space in his Phantom Cruiser along with the masked and caped teenagers, Jan and Jayce, and the monkey known as Blip. The power bands on Space Ghost's wrists as well as his "Invisopower" made the character a memorable addition to the host of animated adventure characters filling the TV

screen. It had a similar flavor to the (then current) primetime series *Jonny Quest*.

Ralph Bakshi's *The Mighty Heroes* (Diaper Man, Cuckoo Man, Rope Man, Strong Man and Tornado Man) fought arch criminals with as much punch as their more serious counterparts. The characters were so well loved, that Bakshi brought them back for a brief reunion in his 1980s TV series, *Mighty Mouse: The New Adventures*.

On other channels, Depatie-Freleng came up with another super group, *The Super Six* (NBC). Elevator Man, Granite Man, Magneto Man, and Super Stretch were heroes for hire who were able to use their skills at transforming to help out The

Animation drawing of Filmation's Batman from the Sixties. ©1991 DC Comics.

Super Service Incorporated. (Also on the show were the adventures of Super Bwoing, a guitar playing detective.) NBC's line-up also included *The Space Kidettes* and *Cool McCool*, a parody about a bumbling secret agent developed by Bob Kane, creator of Batman.

CBS and Filmation intended to capitalize on *Superman*'s popularity and the next season (1967) saw the show expand to an hour and renamed *The Superman Aquaman Hour Of Adventure*. The show now featured two Aquaman adventures, two Superman adventures, a Superboy adventure and a special "guest star" adventure. The "guest star" slot was filled by individual adventures of the Atom, Flash, Hawkman, Green Lantern, the Teen Titans and the Justice League of America. (To avoid possible ethnic problems, Green Lantern's best friend and mechanic had his name changed from "Pieface" to "Cairo.") Each of the "guests" had their own cartoons.

Aquaman rode a seahorse named Storm and his partner Aqualad, often referred to as "Tadpole," had a seahorse named Imp. They were often accompanied on their underwater adventures by a pet walrus named Tusky. Superman found himself fighting an organization known as A.P.E. (Allied Perpetrators of

The Animated Superheroes Of The Sixties

Evil) made up of Lex Luthor, Warlock, Toyman and Prankster.

The following year (1968), the success of the *Batman* TV series had the show block metamorphosing into the *Batman Superman Hour* with a Batman two-parter (echoing the live action series of cliffhangers), a Superman two parter, a single episode of Superboy and a single episode of Batman. Batman confronted a host of his famous villains including Catwoman, Joker, Mr. Freeze, Penguin, Riddler and Mad Hatter. He also faced some newly created menaces like Simon the Pieman, Judge and Dollman. Batgirl popped up to assist Batman and Robin.

Voicing Batman was Olan Soule, a well known radio performer whose meek appearance belied his effective voice. In fact, Soule made a live action appearance on the *Batman* TV series as a newscaster in the first season's "The Curse of King Tut."

In the interests of historical trivia, it should be noted that *The Superman Aquaman Hour Of Adventure* used to have a secret code message, using a "reverse alphabet" code (like Z equals A, X equals B, etc.), which would give a clue as to the next week's guest super hero or adventure. This gimmick only lasted seven weeks and, thanks to the research of Tom McGeehan, here are the

Below:
Space Ghost
© Hanna-Barbera

seven translated coded messages: "Bugs. Frug. Atomic Beat," "Beasts Fallout Teens Fakeout," "Villain Traps Wings Triumph," "Lantern On Star Off," "Bug Bite Flash Lites," "Earth Mixup Heroes Fixup," and "Flowers Fight Power Mite."

Filmation, originally a small studio, rapidly found itself over-committed. They began hiring young and less experienced artists to pick up the slack. In an interview for the book *How to Create Animation*, animator Mark Kausler recalled his time at the studio: "I was called an assistant animator, but at Filmation you really were sort of a Xerox machine operator...A lot of times you didn't even have time to draw Batman or Aquaman. You just took the layouts. Xeroxed two of them. Ripped off the legs, ripped off the arms and literally repositioned them, like cut-out animation. Make a new Xerox of that, strip it up and hand it in. We were under tremendous pressure."

To make things even easier for the new artists, Filmation Xeroxed the official model sheets of the superheroes at a variety of different sizes so that artists could just trace over the face or body they needed at whatever size they needed.

While it seemed as if Filmation had tied up the rights to all the DC

characters, Marvel superheroes arrived on Saturday mornings in a big way the next year (1967) with two series, *Spiderman* and *Fantastic Four,* both on ABC. However, it wasn't the first time the Marvel team had been before the animation camera.

In 1966, while *Superman* debuted on SatAM, Marvel characters were appearing in the world of syndication. (Up to 1966, the only place to see adventure shows was in the syndicated arena on local channels where shows such as *8th Man, Astro Boy, Prince Planet* and *Kimba* aired.) Marvel animation was "born" when Robert Lawrence joined with animators Grant Simmons and Ray Patterson to form the animation company Grantray-Lawrence. They produced *The Marvel Superheroes* in 1966 for the syndication market. It originally appeared on 40 stations. Each show consisted of a three part adventure of either Captain America, The Hulk, Iron Man, The Mighty Thor or Sub-Mariner.

The animation was truly limited in every sense of the word. Most of the animation drawings were taken directly from the Marvel comic books themselves. Offset copies of the artwork were made, word balloons and captions were whited out and backgrounds deleted or changed. Sometimes parts of

hands or heads or other body parts had to be added by the animators because they were cut off in the original comic panel. Then the picture would be jiggled or the camera would zoom in and out or pan across quickly, trying to create the illusion of movement.

In order to get the right pose for a character, drawings often had to be borrowed from other stories that were drawn by other artists, all of whom had distinctive styles that did not match . Unfortunately, this approach created some unexpected problems like having a Steve Ditko-drawn Hulk suddenly become a Bob Powell-drawn Hulk and then a Jack Kirby-drawn

Above:
Underdog
©1967
Leonardo-TTV

Hulk as the character moved through a scene. Since Grantray-Lawrence did a total of 195 individual segments, they also had to borrow stories from *The Fantastic Four* and *The Avengers* comic books and transform them into stories for Sub-Mariner and Captain America. (Additional original adventures of the Sub-Mariner were created by having Doug Wildey, Sparky Moore and other staffers at the studio do sketches that could be used in a similar fashion to the Marvel panels.)

Although now sometimes considered "cult favorites," these cartoons did nothing to enhance the reputation of Marvel and at

Above: Promotional art from Hanna-Barbera's version of The Fantastic Four. ©1991 Marvel.

the time were ridiculed (sometimes on the air by live-action hosts introducing the cartoons). This dismal translation did not dim Marvel's chances, especially with the continued success of Superman on Saturday morning.

Steven Krantz, an independent producer, was responsible for *The Marvel Superheroes* but wanted to improve the package so that it could be sold to the network. He contacted what was left of the Paramount-Famous Studio in New York (the studio that had once produced the Forties Superman cartoons) and Grantray-Lawrence in California to work on a Saturday morning show to be entitled *Spiderman* (without the official hyphen). The Paramount-Famous work showcased the efforts of a young Ralph Bakshi who had been in animation a very short time when this project was assigned to the studio.

The Fall of 1967 saw *Spiderman* premiere. It was different from the other superhero shows that appeared that season. It lacked the clean, antiseptic appearance of the other cartoon factories. There was a roughness and an energy about the show that helped it to achieve a distinctive identity. One of the most memorable things about the show was the theme song, composed by Bob Hanes and Paul Francis Weber. Even two decades later, fans can recite some of the lyrics. ("Spiderman, Spiderman, does whatever a spider can...")

The voices for the show were Canadian. The cast included Bernard Cowan as Spider-Man, Peg Dixon as Betty Brant and Paul Kligman as J. Jonah Jameson.

Determining accurate credit for the shows is difficult because Grantray-Lawrence had a policy that gave credit only to artists who worked full time at their studio. Mike Royer, perhaps best known for his inking of the work of Russ Manning and Jack Kirby or his work in the Disney merchandising department, did a tremendous amount of work on the show but, because he worked at home, his name is absent from the credits.

Only a few of the shows were based on specific Spider-Man adventures from the popular comic books but the shows did make use of many of the same villains such as Kingpin, Dr. Octopus, the Lizard and the Scorpion. (Other less memorable original villainous creations included Boomer and Nitro, Golden Rhino, the Winged Thing, Blotto and Dr. Zap.) Some stories filled the entire half-hour while others were completed in half the time. Attempts were made to keep the wisecracking style that had made the main character a cult hero and, of course, the phrase "friendly neighborhood Spider-man" popped up with alarming frequency.

Unknown to viewers, things started to fall apart quickly behind the scenes. After completing 20 half-hour episodes of *Spiderman*, Grantray-Lawrence went bankrupt

and Krantz and Bakshi were forced to open their own animation studio in New York in order to finish the assignment. Bakshi and his crew of fifteen men had to do the remaining 32 segments of *Spiderman* at the rate of one a week. In order to maintain this insane pace, Bakshi had to reuse as much of the Grantray-Lawrence animation as possible and scenes were padded with Spider-Man swinging endlessly from building to building to building. Cost

Below: Storyboard sequence from "A Prince No More!" Sub-Mariner episode for The Marvel Superheroes *(1966). ©1991 Marvel*

cutting was very much in evidence as Spidey's costume mysteriously lost many of its web lines because they took too much time to add to each drawing.

Bakshi brought comic book artist Gray Morrow to the studio to provide layouts for the series. After the network run, the show enjoyed a healthy run in the syndication market until it was replaced by the new Spider-Man animated show.

On the same morning in 1967 that *Spiderman*

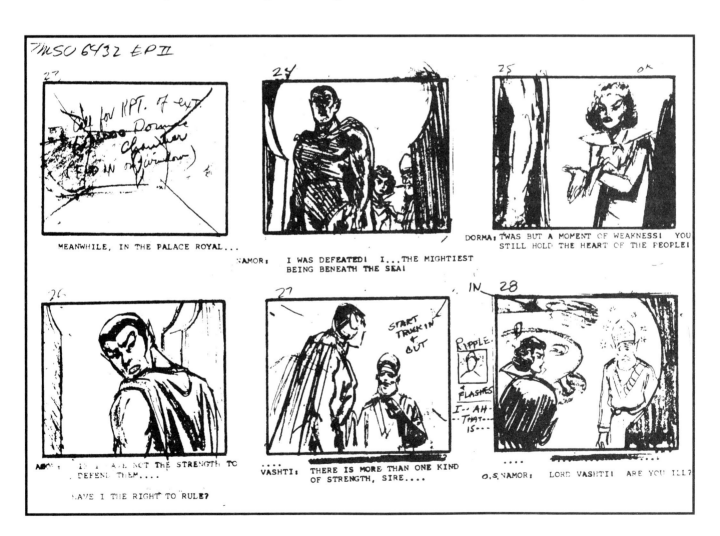

7MSO 6432 EP II

MEANWHILE, IN THE PALACE ROYAL...

NAMOR: I WAS DEFEATED! I...THE MIGHTIEST BEING BENEATH THE SEA!

DORMA: TWAS BUT A MOMENT OF WEAKNESS! YOU STILL HOLD THE HEART OF THE PEOPLE!

NAMOR: I...I ARE NOT THE STRENGTH TO DEFEND THEM....

HAVE I THE RIGHT TO RULE?

VASHTI: THERE IS MORE THAN ONE KIND OF STRENGTH, SIRE....

O.S. NAMOR: LORD VASHTI! ARE YOU ILL?

appeared, earlier in the morning Hanna-Barbera presented their interpretation of Marvel's *Fantastic Four*. This version of Marvel's famous foursome was not greeted with much enthusiasm by the fans. Many of the plots were taken directly from the Marvel comics, but the actual comic book dialogue was eliminated or significantly changed and the action sequences emphasized. It was as if the shows had been drained of all the subtle character interplay and angst that had made the comic so successful.

The show was no different from any of the other Hanna-Barbera superhero shows of the time period. It was characterized by straight-forward action but unlike the comic, not laced with wit or humor. The show did show Reed and Sue sleeping in the same room, but in separate beds.

Gerald Mohr was the voice of Reed Richards, Jo Ann Pflug (pre-*Fall Guy*) was Sue, Jack Flounders was Johnny Storm and Paul Frees (who has voiced animated characters like the Rice Krispies' elves and Boris Badenov) was the Thing. Character design was credited to Alex Toth, a popular comic book artist who would later design the streamlined *Superfriends* also for Hanna-Barbera. Story credit was given to Jack Hanrahan and Phil Hahn.

The episodes were a mixture of adaptations from the comics and original stories. (An interesting trivia note was that since Grantray-Lawrence retained the animation rights to the character of Sub-Mariner at the time, when H-B decided to adapt "Side by Side with the Sub-Mariner" from *Fantastic Four* #33, the character of Prince Namor of Atlantis had to be transformed into Prince Triton of Pacifica. Strangely, Lady Dorma and Attuma were able to retain their own names in both the H-B and G-L versions of the Sub-Mariner stories.)

New to CBS was *Shazzam!*, *The Herculoids* and *Moby Dick And The Mighty Mightor*. *Space Ghost* and *Frankenstein Jr.* returned as well as repeats of the previous prime time *Jonny Quest*. NBC got into full swing with *Samson And Goliath*, *Super President* and *Birdman*. Returning on NBC were *Cool McCool*, *Atom Ant/Secret Squirrel* (their 3rd year). In fact, with all three networks thinking alike, over one-half of all *SatAM* was action/adventure.

Several series of 1967 were more than memorable. Hanna-Barbera struck gold again with *The Mighty Mightor*. It was set in a mythical prehistoric age. A teenage boy named Tor rescued a grateful old hermit who gave the boy a club. When he raised the club to the sky, Tor was transformed into an adult super-strong hero and his pet winged dinosaur became a fire breathing dragon.

DePatie-Freleng entered the superhero era with *Super President* which told of the adventures of the President of the U.S., James Norcross, who secretly had the power to change his molecular structure at will into any gaseous or solid form. Enemies of this country who were too tough for regular law enforcement folks or the military found themselves battling this invincible hero just a few short years after the death of JFK. (Also on the *Super President* show was "Spy Shadow" who in reality was private detective Richard Vance whose shadow could operate independently when it came to solving crimes.) In later years, producer David DePatie spoke harshly about the show claiming it to be one of the worse his company made even though he purposely assigned his "comedy people" to punch up the scripting.

Birdman was another product of Hanna-Barbera. Developed by Alex Toth, the show was based on the escapades of Ray Randall, who was saved from a fiery death by Ra, the Sun god and Hawk deity. Ra gave Ray wings (like Hawkman's) for flight and the ability to shoot "solar ray beams" from his knuckles. A huge

Animation drawing for a planned, but unused, story with Sub-Mariner for The Marvel Superheroes *(1966)*.
©1991 Marvel

The Animated Superheroes Of The Sixties

American eagle named Avenger was his companion as he flew off on missions assigned to him by his chief, Falcon 7. Fans recall his leaping into the air and his echoing yell of his name: "Biiirrrd Man-n-n!" (Later he was teamed with Birdboy.)

1968 found the action/adventure era closing down. The new Fall season saw the number of shows in this category falling to just barely one-third. Though several shows came back (*Spiderman, Fantastic Four, Batman/Superman, Herculoids, Super Six*, its 3rd season, *Birdman* and *Super President*), a new trend began to develop. CBS, who heralded in the action era, now gave a different signal with the debut of such shows as *The Archies, Wacky Races* and *Go-Go Gophers.*

NBC backed down and returned to the successful past of repeats with *Top Cat* (4th year), Flintstones (year 2), and *Underdog* (3rd year, previously on CBS). Oddly, ABC was the lone network to introduce any action shows: *Adventures Of Gulliver* and *Fantastic Voyage.*

1969 found CBS continuing to move to comedy with *Dastardly & Muttley In Their Flying Machine, Perils Of Penelope Pitstop* and *Scooby Doo Where Are You?* all debuting. NBC's newcomers were mostly comedy/repeats with *Here Comes The Grump* and *The Pink Panther* among others. ABC made a few last gallant

tries by going to boys adventures such as *Hot Wheels* and *The Hardy Boys.*

What closed this floodgate of superheroics? It's mostly credited to protests from concerned parents who felt these violent adventures were harming their children. In the late Sixties, the assassinations of Dr. Martin Luther King and of Senator Robert Kennedy sensitized parents to violence in the media. In 1968, the Kerner Commission released their report on the causes and prevention of violence and declared that children's cartoons were a dangerous babysitter. It was an announcement that was supported by other independent surveys such as one done by the *Christian Science Monitor.*

Norm Prescott, then of Filmation, told writer Gary Grossman that "the program-practices departments outlined four major don'ts. No physical violence, no guns, no jeopardy and no threats."

1968, the last major year of action animation on TV was also the year ACT (Action for Children's Television) was formed. It was a group that strongly lobbied for the removal of the violent shows. The outcry was so intense that NBC immediately bought up the contracts for *Birdman* and *Super President* and canceled them in mid-production,

reportedly at a loss of $750,000 to the network. Saturday morning shifted to a comedy-variety format that would be maintained for at least a decade.

Imitation is the sincerest form of television and the networks were filled with super adventures, prompting an embittered Friz Freleng, a former Warner Brothers director and co-owner of DePatie-Freleng, to publicly announce that "You could animate a Superman series on toilet paper and the networks would buy it."

Freleng was correct. The kids wanted superheroes and it was good business to give them superheroes wedged between the toy and cereal commercials. However, when parents protested, it also made good business sense to count the profits from the last three years and to quietly retreat into the land of unfunny humor.

The age of heroes came to an end but the memory of that time is still strong. That era of action animation, long gone from the tube remains a well loved memory to most of those who grew up during those years. Three years when superheroes flew and fought for truth, justice and higher ratings.

TOP SECRET

CHAPTER THREE:

SEX AND CENSORSHIP IN ANIMATION

Sex And Censorship In Animation

"He couldn't take my boop-oop-a-doop away!" proclaimed cartoon flapper Betty Boop in the 1932 cartoon *Boop Oop A Doop*. Audiences of the Thirties knew that phrase was a veiled sexual reference. Within a few short years censors finally accomplished what a host of lecherous cartoon characters couldn't. Censors would take away Betty's "boop."

Cartoon censorship has existed nearly as long as the cartoons themselves. The only difference is the way in which the material is controlled. In the 1920s, middle America was allegedly outraged by the tales of excesses and debauchery in the Hollywood community and the films they made. In order to forestall government intervention to censor films, Hollywood established its own censorship board headed by Will Hays. The Hays Office immediately set about cleaning up Hollywood's act and started strictly enforcing restrictions so that films would not tend "to shock, insult, or offend the community or outrage public morals and decency."

Betty Boop was one of the first cartoon characters to feel the wrath of the Hays Office. In 1934, Paramount Pictures, the studio releasing the Fleischer Betty Boop cartoons announced that "Betty Boop, a Paramount star, the 'It' girl of

Below:
Betty Boop shows her garter and panties.
© 1991 King Features

Cartoonland...was sixteen years old when she was born on April 1st three years ago, and celebrates her sixteenth birthday every year... She is the only screen star who possesses eternal youth." (The reference to the "It girl" was an allusion to live action silent film star Clara Bow,

who was referred to as the "It girl" with "It" being sex appeal.)

For a sixteen year old, Betty certainly had a lot of adventures. In *Boop Oop A Doop* (1932) and *Betty Boop's Big Boss* (1935), both of her bosses rub her breasts as a prelude to a fate worse than death in those days. Television syndication prints have trimmed or eliminated those interesting moments as well as such moments in shorts like *Poor Cinderella* (1934) and *Silly Scandals* (1931) where her top kept falling down to reveal a lacy bra.

Betty was not shy; she danced a topless hula in *Betty Boop's Bamboo Isle* (1932) with a flower lei barely hiding her charms. When she recreated that moment in *Betty Boop's Rise To Fame* in 1934, her bare breast actually flashes the audience for less than a second. Some scenes that remain in televised prints do include a flash of underwear or a wiggle that would have given even Mae West or Madonna pause.

In 1934, the Production Code took full effect and Betty was one of the first victims. After all, Betty's *Red Hot Mama* (1934) was rejected by the British Board of Censors and was not allowed to be screened in England. Betty was transformed into a conservative young homemaker, complete with apron. Her wild friends and adventures disappeared, replaced by relatives like Grampy and more domestic escapades like trying to get rid of a pesky fly who is bothering her in the kitchen. It was no surprise that when the last official Betty Boop cartoon was released in 1939 that it didn't even feature Betty.

(When the Fleischer Studio moved down to Florida, for fun the animators put together a private porno reel. According to Fleischer historian Leslie Carbaga, one sequence shows an animated Betty sexually assaulting Popeye.)

Other characters were also affected, but none to the extreme of Betty. (But then, few characters had been as outrageous as Ms. Boop.) For example, Walt Disney toned down most of the barnyard humor of Mickey Mouse. Scenes of Mickey physically abusing farm animals, such as when he yanks on piglets, attached to their mothers breasts, to make music in *Steamboat Willie* (1927) were reduced (and physically cut out in some prints). Few recall the racier, more Earthy Mickey of the late Twenties and early Thirties. Between the watchful eyes of the Hays office, which administered the Production Code, and the growing popularity of Mickey as a children's character and corporate image, Mickey was

also toned down.

Most studios, though, merely had to contend with the notion of having scenes cut, or shortened. An issue of *Look* magazine from 1939 featured a five page article entitled "Hollywood Censors Its Animated Cartoons." It focused solely on the output from Warner Brothers.

"Robert Taylor may kiss Garbo in a feature picture, but it isn't considered nice for Porky Pig to kiss Petunia Pig in an animated cartoon" stated the article as it gave many specific examples of how censorship was more restrictive for cartoons than live action feature films. According to the article, one scene in *Speaking Of The Weather* (1937) featured a caricature of actor William Powell taking his dog for a walk and the dog's desire to do what a dog does on a walk. The scene was meant to parody a similar live action moment from one of Powell's *Thin Man* films. As originally drawn, the scene was supposedly long but "when the censors finished little remained" except a shot of the dog stopping by a fire hydrant and then a quick cut to a reaction on the man's face.

Warners also had to censor its mermaid character in *Mr. And Mrs. Is The Name* (1935) by lengthening her hair to cover her topless breasts, although some topless moments did seem to slip by the censors somehow.

Right: Rejected and revised version of mermaid from Mr. And Mrs. Is The Name *(1935). © 1991 Warner Brothers*

Sex And Censorship In Animation

Above: Animator Preston Blair later used his animation for Tex Avery's infamous Red as an example of strutting in the Walter Foster book Animation. *© 1949 Preston Blair and Walter Foster*

Also removed was the mermaid's navel.

As Warner's director Bob Clampett stated, "Things like that hurt the films greatly if you knew what was there originally. You got so sick of that sort of thing sometimes you'd say, 'Well, I'll put something worse in there, something obvious for them to censor.' And that was the thing that they would let go through."

Clampett was notorious for slipping in such material. One such gag was in a Warners short he directed in 1943, *An Itch In Time.* A helpless dog under attack from a very aggressive flea tries to relieve the pain by frantically rubbing his butt all over the room. The dog stops for a brief moment to tell the audience, "Hey, I better cut this out! I might get to like it!" This masturbation reference not only got past the censors but remains even in the edited Warners prints on television today.

Many of those who worked on the classic cartoons have stated time and again that their films were made for adults, not children. This statement does not to seem to be in complete agreement with others at the time. Including the producers and the Hays Office.

Warner's producer Leon Schlesinger publicly supported the Hays Office restrictions and stated in the late Thirties that "We cannot forget that while the cartoon today is excellent entertainment for young and old, it is primarily the favorite motion picture fare of children. Hence we always must keep their best interests at heart by making our product proper for the impressionable minds."

To the Hays Office and most producers, the major topic to avoid was "s-e-x."

For some reason, cartoon makers couldn't get their minds off it! One of Tex Avery's most loved creations was the sexy Red (Hot Riding Hood). Warners' Pepe LePew was one of the most insistently romantic characters ever created. Bugs Bunny cross dressed. Daffy Duck wanted to date human female movie stars. An animated Humphrey Bogart even shoots a wolf over Lauren Bacall's butt (of her cigarette). These were considered safe and harmless.

Other actions were not so lightly taken, especially the baring of breasts. Betty Boop had hinted at it. Warners' mermaid, mentioned above, was part of a cartoon cover-up. Even Disney crossed the line with *Fantasia*'s centaurettes. Appearing in the "Pastoral Symphony" sequence, they were originally intended to be topless. Preliminary artwork and model sheets feature them that way. However, instead of classic, elegant creatures, they resemble young bobby-soxer teenagers of the time. Obviously this was a contributing factor to hiding the bare breasts of these mythological creatures. Some brief moments of toplessness still appears at the opening of the sequence when the centaurettes are at the pool.

When the Hays Office eventually disbanded, films were allowed greater freedom in subject matter and presentation. By then, most of the studios had dropped their cartoon departments. The only major theatrical animation was the Disney features. It was quite awhile before there was a notable exception. *Fritz The Cat* (1971) was an animated feature directed by Ralph Bakshi that was advertised as being "X-rated and animated." (X-rated cartoons were not new, but they usually were done for private screenings and did not receive wide public theatrical release.) Loosely based on the popular underground comix character created by Robert Crumb, the film had typical funny animals doing drugs, having sex and generally participating in activities associated with the hippies of the Sixties.

Not even animators were always ready to break the X-barrier. Bakshi said the animators who didn't work out on *Fritz* were of two types. There were the ones who came in with a leer "wanting to be very dirty and draw filthy pictures." Then there were those who were too prudish and "not with it enough to draw reality." At first, several animators left. A female cartoonist walked out because she couldn't bring herself to draw an exposed nipple; another woman assistant quit because she couldn't explain to her children what she was doing. Still another cartoonist quit because he couldn't draw a Black crow shooting a pig cop.

In Bakshi's view, animators who quit merely showed their own sexual hang-ups. When animators asked whether the sex scenes were in good taste, Bakshi would reply, "Would you call a cat that chases a crow into a junk yard to (have sex with) her, good taste?" The success of *Fritz* launched

MISS "X"

*Left:
Walter Lantz's entry into cartoon cheesecake was this lady, originally called "Miss X," from Great Man In Siam.
© 1991 Walter Lantz Productions*

Sex And Censorship In Animation

caricatures of African-American people, a staple of humor before the Sixties. Bob Clampett's *Coal Black And The Seben Dwarfs* (1942), a parody of Disney's famous feature, is now only seen at special retrospectives. Tex Avery's *All This And Rabbit Stew* (1941) had a little African-American boy hunting Bugs Bunny and losing everything he owns in a crap game with the wily rabbit. Even the most devoted Popeye fan may never get a chance to see *Pop-Pie Ala Mode* (1945) where the famous sailor is rescued by some stereotyped cannibals.

Chuck Jones and his crew at MGM took the old Tom and Jerry theatrical shorts that featured Mammy Two Shoes, the African-American maid who was only seen from the knees down, and had to animate new white legs over her chubby black legs. Phil Roman, one of those who did the new legs, remembers that, "We were brought in and spent days rotoscoping and re-animating the legs so that they would be thin and white; not thick and black. When we asked what they would do about the (ethnic) accent, they told us they were going to put a funny Irish voice in. We guessed it was all right to make fun of the Irish!"

It's odd to watch many of these shorts on television. Evidently tracks and prints have been mixed creating

Bakshi's career and notoriety and inspired a less well received sequel (not directed by Bakshi).

With the theatrical barriers broken, the only place cartoons need fear was television. When the studios started selling their theatrical cartoons to television, it was merely more product to fill the vast wasteland. Kids coming home from school could enjoy all the racist, violent, sexually suggestive moments that had amused their parents in theaters.

When television started to come under scrutiny, so did these repeated animated antics. The quickest to vacate the air were those considered racist. In the more racially

Above:
A scene from Ralph Bakshi's autobiographical animated feature, Heavy Traffic (1973), is one of the few commercial uses of sex and ethnic caricatures in post code animation.
© 1973 American International Pictures

sensitive times of the late Fifties and Sixties, studios and networks began to take steps to eliminate those moments and sometimes complete films that showed what was considered "unhealthy" or "dehumanized" stereotypes.

The first ones noted were those with Black caricatures. Long a popular ethnic character in stage shows, comic strips and live action films, animation followed suit with its various happy maids, friendly slaves, singing and dancing boys and more.

Those cartoons soon disappeared from syndication packages along with any exaggerated odd sights. One short features the original Black legs, but a young (White) girl's voice. Others can feature the white legs, but the ethnic voice. Luckily on home video, the original legs and voice are intact.

Many early Disney shorts contain references to Black caricatures from *Mickey's Man Friday* (1935), where he meets natives on a tropical island, to *Tea For Two Hundred* (1948), where Donald is tormented by a tribe of ethnic ants. Disney is still frequently criticized for the crows in *Dumbo* (1941) and the portrayal of the live action Uncle Remus in *Song Of The South* (1946).

On occasion, Disney attempted to correct such material. In *Fantasia*, the "Pastoral Symphony" has an extreme African-American female caricature who does servile duties like decorating a tail, polishing hooves and assisting Bacchus to sit down.

These scenes were cut out which played havoc with the music track. For the 1990 re-release, some scenes were enlarged so the caricatures were "out of frame." Other scenes ended up being replaced with different scenes from the film also reframed. Some audiences and critics still complained about a brief on screen appearance of the zebra centaurettes.

Other ethnic stereotypes weren't ignored by cartoons.

In the original animated version of *The Three Little Pigs* (1933), there is an unflattering Jewish peddler caricature that the wolf assumes in an attempt to trick the pigs. Today, viewers will not find that scene because that section was reanimated in later years by the Disney staff to eliminate that offensive moment and the wolf is now merely a brush salesman. Donald Duck director Jack Hannah was involved with the re-animation. However, sharp-eyed viewers can still see a very brief glimpse of a Jewish caricature mouse in *The Brave Little Tailor* (1938), a caricature that was repeated in the comic strip version of the story.

There were many World

Below:
One of the several censored scenes in Fantasia *no longer found in release prints.*
© 1991 Walt Disney Company

War II cartoons that, in the spirit of the time in which they were made, dehumanized Japanese, German and Italian people. Popeye destroys a Japanese fleet in *You're A Sap, Mr. Jap* (1942). Bugs Bunny gives equal battle in *Bugs Bunny Nips The Nips* (1943) where the wily hare hands out grenades disguised as ice cream bars. "Here you go, monkey face," Bugs tells one of the Japanese soldiers. These cartoons have largely been pulled from distribution.

Not so easily identified and isolated was the violence in these classic cartoons. Most of them had gotten their biggest laughs thanks to guns, explosions, knives and axes.

Sex And Censorship In Animation

"It's frightening," said Charles Bronson in a 1978 interview. "I watched a Road Runner cartoon with my little girl. They dropped a rock on the coyote and flattened him, but he popped right up again. That's really shocking to me because when a child grows up with that sort of thing, he'll feel he can go around hitting people on the head with a hammer and they'll be all right.

Bronson is best known for his role in violent films like *The Magnificent Seven* and the *Death Wish* series. "The difference between someone seeing *Death Wish* and my child seeing a violent cartoon is the age," continued Bronson. "My movies are rated and the people who see them are not children. *Death Wish* wasn't that extreme. It was clean violence. When I shot a man, he was shot and that was the end of it."

It was reactions like that which resulted in many of the Warner Brothers cartoons appearing on television having scenes cut. Children no longer saw Elmer Fudd aim a gun at Daffy Duck, fire the gun and see Daffy's bill spin around his face. On Saturday morning, the scene of the gun firing was usually cut, leaving a confused child to see a gun being pointed and suddenly the bill spinning. In the recent release syndication package, instead of eliminating entirely the

moment, the scene now shifts to a frozen frame from another scene in the cartoon while the action is heard off screen.

A former employee at Warners talks of a card file in which each Warners short has a card. On that card are scenes in the film that are considered inappropriate. It was easy to see that as the years had gone on, more things had been placed on the cards.

When producers began making cartoons for television they found the rules were very different than making cartoons for the theaters. At a film studio, the producer only had to worry about budgets, time schedules and "naughty" material. In television there were network executives and sponsors.

Bob Clampett found that this group was as unpredictable as any Hays Office. After producing an Emmy winning puppet show, *Time For Beany*, during the Fifties, he produced an animated version in the early Sixties and ran into the same battles he'd had at Warners. "They'd see a cartoon like *Beanyland* and they'd say 'Oh, you can't have that caricature of Walt Disney in there saying he'll make this his Dismal Land,'" remarked Clampett in an interview. "I'd say, 'Where's Walt Disney in there? The character in there with the hook nose and moustache is

my long time villain Dishonest John. Everyone knows that.' Everyone except the people running the cartoons on television."

Another time, Clampett had Dishonest John packaging the moon as cheese and bringing it back to Earth to sell it. "I had the word 'KRAFTY' on the package and ABC was afraid Kraft Cheese would sue them. It was those kind of things they censored," laughed Clampett.

So, like in his Warners cartoons, Clampett would start to add outrageous things for the network to remove and leave the rest of the cartoon alone. Once again, the watchdogs would let some of the more outrageous things slip by them. "In my Snorky cartoon, *There's No Such Thing As A Sea Serpent*, for which I wrote all the lyrics, I had a sequence with several prehistoric creatures called triceratops, singing 'All triceratops that try Sarah say she's tops.' Lines like that are still there with the Censors' Good Housekeeping Seal of Approval," stated Clampett.

Jay Ward, responsible for characters like Bullwinkle Moose, George of the Jungle and others, was also not immune to censorship problems. There was one episode of Dudley Do-Right that reportedly only aired on network television once. The short was known as "Stokey the Bear" about a seven hundred pound light brown bear who wore a Mountie hat. Obviously a parody of famed fire fighting symbol Smokey the Bear, Stokey had been hypnotized by Snidely Whiplash to start fires instead of putting them out. The U.S. Forestry Service saw no humor in a thinly veiled parody of their famous bear setting a fire station on fire and starting the great Chicago blaze blamed on Mrs. O'Leary's cow. They filed a formal complaint with NBC and the segment was withdrawn from being rerun.

Some of Ward's naughtiness did slip through. In the *Fractured Fairy Tales* Sleeping Beauty parody, the prince admitted he was a "hog flogger," a term related to male masturbation.

The largest change in animation production came in the Sixties. With a growing cultural awareness and a ratings war on Saturday morning some individuals began to pay greater attention to the unsavory elements. One of these individuals was Peggy Charren. When she decided to watch some cartoons with her four year old daughter she soon discovered in her own words that "all they had for children were wall-to-wall monster cartoons."

In 1968, Charren founded Action for Children's Television (ACT) with three friends who also had young children. Today the group operates out of a small office on an annual budget of around $175,000 and a paid staff of four, including Charren who receives a $35,000 salary. There are over 10,000 members around the country and over the years ACT has formed ties with groups like the American Academy of Pediatrics, the National Education Association, the National P.T.A. and many religious organizations. ACT's lobbying and legal challenges have resulted in such things as the Federal Communications Commission's ban of advertising by hosts of children's programs and the Federal Trade Commission's prohibiting vitamin advertising on children's programs. Charren told the *New York Times* in 1991 that "(President) Reagan decimated children's television" when he deregulated the broadcasting industry.

ACT's threat of applying pressure has been enough to make studios and networks even more cautious about anything that might be considered questionable. Though some question the full strength of ACT, none dare overestimate the power of a nebulous monster known as the Standards and Practice (S&P) department at each network.

While the networks claim they don't really "censor" anything, S&P watches over animation and live action to make every effort to assure the work is responsible. All networks state they have the same standards for all shows, whether aired on Saturday morning or Saturday night. The problem dealing with S&P is that with no real guidelines, most decisions seem arbitrary. The list of bizarre decisions by S&P is endless.

A key difference between a group like ACT and S&P is that a watchdog group can only act after a film or show has aired. S&P is usually in from the beginning. They may review the scripts, the storyboards, the audio recordings from the actor's voice session and more. It is their task to nip any possible problem in the toon.

Standards and Practices will censor acts that they feel might be imitated by children. It was believed that children could not understand the very real, and often deadly consequences of an act performed in a cartoon. Rather than risk any mishap and possible lawsuit, S&P would continually stress a cautious, conservative approach to all problems.

Even a supposedly bland show like *The Smurfs* was not safe from change. Peyo, the creator of the little blue elves, commented that when his long running comic book series was translated to television at least one familiar element was changed by Hanna-Barbera's concern about S&P. "I had to do away with a trademark of most stories: the bespectacled Smurf who hits the moralizing Smurf on the head with a mallet as soon as the moralizing begins, even some peace-loving people have their squabbles. That couldn't be shown on T.V. I was told because the little spectator could very well go into his father's garage, take a hammer and hit his sister on the head with it."

The late Norman Maurer was a storyman for several Hanna-Barbera productions who ran into unusual rulings. In *Josie And The Pussycats,* he wrote a scene in which a pussycat, escaping from a science fiction menace, took refuge in a dish of spaghetti. CBS disallowed it. "Kids'll put their cats in spaghetti," Maurer was told. He wrote a scene where the character was going to deliver a little message at the end of the show about the undesirability of dictators such as Caesar, Napoleon and Hitler. Hitler had to be eliminated from the list because using Hitler's image might offend people. ABC's Office of Standard and Practices took exception to Maurer having DynoMutt using the phrase "guys and gals;" young ladies, Maurer was informed very clearly, should always be referred to as "girls."

In 1980, Filmation Studio circulated the following memo to its staff: "Program Practices at CBS has ruled that a character that has been hit or in a fight **Can not** have: (1) eyes at halfmast (2) eyes twirling (3) tongue hanging out (4) dazed or hurt look (5) closed eyes (6) circle of stars around head. **No Expression Of Pain Or Dazed Expression!** The characters **Can** react with frustration or anger at having been foiled again. **Camera:** Do not shoot scenes you find with the no-no's in them!"

In the Eighties, more and more watchdog groups have come to the forefront. Most of these state they are associated with religious groups and beliefs. These self-proclaimed protectors of society have seen evil in cartoons that the general public apparently missed. Phil Phillips, the author of *Turmoil of the Toybox,* gets specific on how Satan is gaining control of children's minds. He details that the unicorns in *My Little Pony* are symbolic of the Antichrist, that Care Bears promote Eastern religious philosophy and that Papa Smurf uses spells and incantations. According to Phillips, one of the worse offenders is *He-Man And The Masters Of The Universe* because the concept usurps God's role as the actual master of the universe.

It is not easy to dismiss some of the more vocal critics. In 1988, Reverend Donald Wildmon, head of a media watch group called American Family Association, claimed that Mighty Mouse was a cocaine addict. An episode of the TV series *Mighty Mouse: The New Adventures* entitled "The Little Tramp" featured the World's Mightiest Mouse sniffing the crushed remains of a flower he had been given earlier in the story and his mood changed dramatically. Wildmon claimed it was a hidden reference to cocaine and to fortify his argument he pointed out that the producer of the show was Ralph Bakshi, "a known pornographer."

The protests continued and finally much to the surprise and disappointment of many people, Ralph Bakshi edited out the offending three and a half seconds. Bakshi explained, "I attended the High School for Industrial Arts in Brooklyn. I remember teachers who quit. Because of McCarthyism, they weren't able to teach what they wanted. This is the same thing. Mighty Mouse was happy after smelling the flowers because it helped him remember the little girl who sold it to him fondly. But even if you're right, their accusations become part of the air we breathe. That's why I cut the scene. I can't have children wondering if Mighty Mouse is using cocaine." (Bakshi claimed these missing seconds would be found in the original short when the series went to home video.)

"This is a de facto admission that indeed Mighty Mouse was snorting cocaine," claimed Wildmon. "We have been vindicated by CBS, itself."

Such "vindication" only makes producers more wary. Not wishing to frighten children or offend parent groups, Steven Spielberg trimmed scenes and cut out whole sequences from his animated features *An American Tail* (1984) and *The Land Before Time* (1986). Scenes trimmed in *Tail* included the first look at America for the mice (one character was considered to be "too Jewish"), and the monster wave sequence (considered "too scary"). *Land* had a number of the dinosaur battle scenes shortened. Over ten minutes were cut from the original running time.

After receiving criticism about *All Dogs Go To Heaven* (1989), Don Bluth, who directed Spielberg's first two pictures, now has his films viewed by various groups. They help to make sure any scenes too frightening, questionable or suggestive are deleted. His upcoming *Rock-A-Doodle* had the female lead's design changed halfway through production because she was deemed too sexy.

When we hear of foreign

governments banning films and cartoons, it is usually taken lightly. The reasons for the ban seem almost funny. In 1979, Philippine President Ferdinand Marcos ordered the removal from Philippine television all of the Japanese cartoon shows about futuristic robots. He felt the shows were extremely war-like and were having a harmful effect on children. Besides, they were programmed at a time when children were supposed to be doing homework.

Even Walt Disney and his creations have felt the wrath of these censors. In the Seventies, one African nation banned the original version

Below: Storyboard drawing of Donald Duck from Der Fuehrer's Face. © 1991 Walt Disney Company

of *The Rescuers* (1977). The reason was that Bernard says, upon finding a giant diamond, "Holy smoke, that's it." The nation considered it an effrontery to religion. Most U.S. viewers smiled at such action over a harmless phrase.

Everyone got a good laugh in the early Eighties when Finland decided to ban Donald Duck. The youth board, which made its decision unanimously, found that the famous Duck was unduly bourgeois, presented destructive attitudes toward society and was not suitable for children. For evidence, the board cited pictures of naked ducks, tales of

Sex And Censorship In Animation

Even Cinema Cartoons Must Pass Censor's Inspection ·

BEFORE   **AFTER**

HOLLYWOOD, Calif., May 18 (AP). —Movie cartoons are subjected to as many "must nots" as feature pictures with human characters. Every one of the 200-odd cartoons made every year (by nine companies) must be submitted to the Hays office for moral inspection.

Leon Schlesinger, who makes the Looney Tunes, finds that the children who see his pictures invariably make reports to their parents. And the parents, very often, make reports to him. Censorship is what it amounts to.

He doesn't use scarey characters any more because, in one picture, he had a monster that was the heavy. The monster frightened the children —as well as Porky the Pig—and the letters of protest looked like a star's fan mail. He's found out, too, that it is very dangerous to kid dialects.

Schlesinger's pictures have run afoul of the official censors only once. One of his artists didn't put enough grass on a hula dancer's skirt. All of the scenes of the dancer had to be remade . . . with considerably more skirt. Once his animators forgot to put skirts on the lady pig—a natural slip—and one that wasn't noticed until Schlesinger's stenographers looked at the picture. They wrote memos to the boss about it.

—

*Left:
1937 article on censorship problems on Warner cartoons. Not the mention of "scary" monsters and not "enough grass" on the dancer.*

*Right:
Typical stereotype of the early Thirties. From Warner's Hittin' The Trail For Hallelujah Land (1931). © Warner Brothers*

incomplete families, harmful attitudes toward children, and what they claimed was Donald's common law marriage to Daisy Duck.

How really distant are we from such thinking? The producers of *The Simpsons* were given a special tour of the San Onofre nuclear power plant (in San Clemente, California) by the U.S. Council for Energy Awareness, an industry information group. The producers decided to no longer make fun about the safety at the nuclear power plant where Homer works. "No more three-eyed fish," proclaimed *Simpsons* producer Sam Simon.

A campaign has started to have stations stop showing *Tiny Toon Adventures* featuring Shirley The Loon. The character, a duck parody of Shirley MacLaine, practices New Age religion (which many claim is a combination of the occult, Shamanism, witchcraft and mysticism). The protesters say showing children alternate religions to Christianity is wrong.

A Saturday morning series' script features a funny car ride with a reckless taxi driver. The network requests that the driver of the taxi not resemble any minority.

An animator on a commercial tells of how the hook on the back of a cartoon pick-up truck had to be re-drawn because it looked too much like a sickle. "I asked why and was told the agency was afraid it might offend people with sickle cell anemia. I said, 'Boy, they really had to reach for that one!'" laughed the animator.

Sadly, for those who just want to enjoy cartoons, someone will always be reaching...and taking away.

**CAP'N
CRUNCH**

IN THE CENTER OF THE EARTH

TOP SECRET

CHAPTER FOUR:

SNAP!
CRACKLE!
CARTOONS!

Snap! Crackle! Cartoons!

Sneakily appearing during station breaks, like some form of subliminal message, some of the best loved and remembered animated characters have lived happily for years. Though they weren't stars of TV series or major feature films, these animated heroes have enjoyed many of the perks granted their more legitimate counterparts. They were made into toys and games, appeared in comics and became a part of U.S. culture.

From Speedy Alka Seltzer to Chester Cheetah, this specialized group of cartoon superstars are often better remembered than their historical counterparts who did appear in feature films or TV series. These characters are no second class performers having been animated by some of the top studios including Disney, Hanna-Barbera and Jay Ward.

Theaters had shown animated commercials for decades, in fact puppet animator/movie producer, George Pal began his career creating animated commercials for theaters. The invasion of TV into U.S. homes brought about a new breed of animated commercial. More than just a commercial that had been animated, these ads starred a distinctive character keyed to be identified with a particular product. One area that was targeted by sponsors was the fast

growing children's cereal market.

Kids were the new kings of the breakfast table as the world sped up and the traditional family breakfast became a thing of the past. While fathers rushed off for a quick commute to work and mothers started to enter the job market and teenagers worried about their figures, there was only time for a fast and easy to prepare breakfast which was primarily devoured by small children before they made the unwilling trek to school.

What better way to capture the hearts and minds of our youth than to use the device that had been so successful in holding their attention for nearly half a century, children's programming. During the golden days of radio, "kid's shows" such as *Superman* and *The Lone Ranger* were sponsored by a variety of cereals ranging from Cheerios to Pep. When such shows moved to the world of TV, it was not unusual for the live action star of the show to step into the commercial and recommend the product. As the Fifties progressed, though, more and more children's programming was becoming animated, either by the repeats of theatrical shorts (often with a live, local host) or the newer animated shorts and serials (such as *Crusader Rabbit* and *Ruff And Reddy*).

In the Fifties and Sixties,

there were no real guidelines for commercials. Special effects could be added without restriction to make things faster, bigger, brighter or more realistic. Claims that a product could improve a person's social life or health or grant special powers or sex appeal would go unchallenged. ACT (Action for Children's Television) was formed in the late 1960's and created a lot of noise about advertising on children's shows, and there was always the isolated "minority group" that might become vocal. However, it wasn't until 1977 that the Children's Advertising Review Unit was established by the Council of Better Business Bureaus to require regulations and guidelines for sponsors.

In the free-for-all Fifties, one of the first firms to stake a claim in the animated world of cereal commercials was the grand-daddy of all cold cereal companies, Kellogg's. Today's health conscious parents might blanch with horror when confronted with some of these ads including ones featuring Sugar Pops Pete's smiling statement that Sugar Pops cereal (originally called Sugar Corn Pops) was "shot with sugar through and through." It was certainly a dietary choice guaranteed to wake up even the most sluggish child before sending the hyper little human into the unsuspecting clutches of disciplinary teachers.

Sugar Pops Pete was a prairie dog in a cowboy hat who often used a candy cane striped six shooter to "pop" a bad guy like Billy the Kidder full of sugar and magically transform the grump into a better person who was as sweet as the cereal. Pete inherited the spokesman position from the live action TV cowboy heroes Wild Bill Hickock and his over weight sidekick, Jingles, which probably accounted for Pete wearing a ten gallon hat, having a gun and holster and enjoying adventures in the Wild West.

Pete was one of the most successful cereal salesmen whose jingle, "Sugar Pops are tops!," brings back many fond memories for baby boomers. He was just one of dozens of animated animals that represented products for children. Advertising executives had discovered that animals had a high recognition factor with children and were often perceived as more "friendly" than real people. Like many other characters, product changes and changing tastes eventually brought an end to Pete's illustrious career.

Sugar Pops, was a product of Kellogg's, one of the kings of breakfast cereal companies and the creator of a host of memorable animated spokesmen from Battle Creek, Michigan. For a generation of youngsters, Battle Creek was the magical home of marvelous "free" prizes available by sending box tops from cereals. In fact, Battle Creek is the home for cold cereals.

Most people don't realize that breakfast cereals, as they are known today, are less than 100 years old and they all began accidentally thanks to a man named Kellogg. In 1876, Dr. John Harvey Kellogg was hired to run the Battle Creek Sanitarium in Michigan. The diet he prescribed for patients was strictly vegetarian so he experimented with new concoctions to make that regiment more palatable.

One experiment involved running boiled wheat dough through rollers, having it become sheets before it was toasted and ground into flour. In 1895, Kellogg was called away on an emergency and left the pans of dough sitting out for a while. When he returned to run it through the rollers, he got flakes instead of sheets. He toasted them anyway and the patients loved them. Later the staff developed two variations which resulted in rice flakes and corn flakes.

Kellogg, along with his brother William, opened the Sanitarium Health Food Company to sell the flakes to the general public. They sold over 100,000 pounds of them in the first year causing 42 Battle Creek based cereal companies to spring up in an attempt to capitalize on Kellogg's success and the reputation of the area.

Brother William had been quietly buying up stock until he was able to take control of the company in 1906 and thus alienating his more medically minded brother who refused to talk to him again until his death in 1942. William renamed the company the Kellogg Toasted Corn Flakes Company and by 1909, the firm was selling more than a million cases a year.

William K. Kellogg, whose signature appears on every Kellogg's cereal box, died at the age of 92 in 1951, leaving a five billion dollar dried breakfast cereal business to his heirs. Neither brother saw the influx of television advertising that would generate characters like Snap, Crackle and Pop or Tony the Tiger who became as well known as any feature film or television star.

Tony the Tiger in his 1955 debut roared that Sugar Frosted Flakes were "Gr-r-r-reat!" Tony was designed by a children's book illustrator, Martin Provensen, and like most long lived animated characters, his crude original appearance underwent a series of changes until he became more appealing and fatherly.

In his original appearances, he was only about seven inches tall and simply popped out from his image on his cereal box.

Snap! Crackle! Cartoons!

Today's Tony is closer in size to a real tiger, approximately six and half feet tall. He became a family man and teamed with a child tiger, originally called simply "boy" or "son" but eventually christened Tony, Jr. and who was given the job of selling the now defunct Frosted Rice. (Kellogg's later introduced the same cereal as Frosted Rice Krispies with Snap, Crackle and Pop as the hawkers.)

Tony was one of the first animated cereal heroes to be rotoscoped into live action situations and interact with real people and objects. Truly, he was and still is the king of the Kellogg's characters but as he's grown older, his early slapstick antics have now mellowed so he is more of an understanding, helpful bystander giving paternal advice to eat more Frosted Flakes. Certainly helping Tony 's popularity was his rich, distinctive voice supplied by Thurl Ravenscroft.

Snap, Crackle and Pop are cute little cereal elves who also made their debut in the mid-Fifties to sing the praises of Rice Krispies. Like Tony, their original design was by an illustrator of children's books, W.T. Grant, and like Tony, their appearance was softened over the years. Other than their hair color and costumes, as far as the public

Above:
Original closing credits to The Huckleberry Hound Show featured Huck and the Kellogg's characters.
©1991 Kellogg's
©1991 Hanna-Barbera

Opposite page: Huck and Yogi hawk Kellogg's Corn Flakes in a '50s comic book ad.
©1991 Kellogg's
©1991 Hanna-Barbera

was concerned their personalities were pretty much interchangeable. Over three decades later, they still successfully sell the noisiest of breakfast cereals which has grown to a line of several "variations" including the above mentioned Frosted Rice Krispies.

Another longtime Kellogg's favorite is Toucan Sam. Sounding like Ronald Colman, Sam sniffs out Fruit Loops for a variety of guest characters. In the original commercials, he spoke largely in pig-Latin, frequently looking for "Oot-fray, Oops-lay" (Fruit Loops). Today he has joined the ranks of characters who seem more interested in tempting cereal and sugar addicts. However, like Sugar Pops Pete, not all cereal spokesmen (or even cereals for that matter) last forever . Coco, a talking monkey, reminded audiences that Cocoa Krispies "tastes like a chocolate milkshake, only

crunchy." He was replaced by Hanna-Barbera's Snagglepuss for a brief period. The cereal later became promoted as just another variation of Rice Krispies. By the early Nineties, Coco had returned on the box and animated commercials now singing a reggae-style tune.

Smaxie the seal advertised Sugar Smacks in the cereal's earliest days. The next best remembered character was Dig 'Em Frog. He continued on through a change in names to Honey Smacks. For a brief two box appearance in the late-Eighties, a bear named Wally was brought into the spotlight to emphasize the honey in the name. Dig 'Em was right back though. In the early Nineties, Dig 'Em's raspy voice was smoothed out a bit and he stopped giving all the kids "five." Taking a leaf from Sugar Bear's book, he began having more standard animated adventures trying to get the Honey Smacks from some adversary.

The famous team of Hanna and Barbera were particularly grateful for Kellogg's cereals which fully sponsored H-B's first three syndicate TV shows: *Huckleberry Hound* (1958), *Quick Draw McGraw* (1959) and *Yogi Bear* (1961). Early baby boomers may even vaguely recall the ending credits of *Huckleberry Hound* where a runaway jalopy

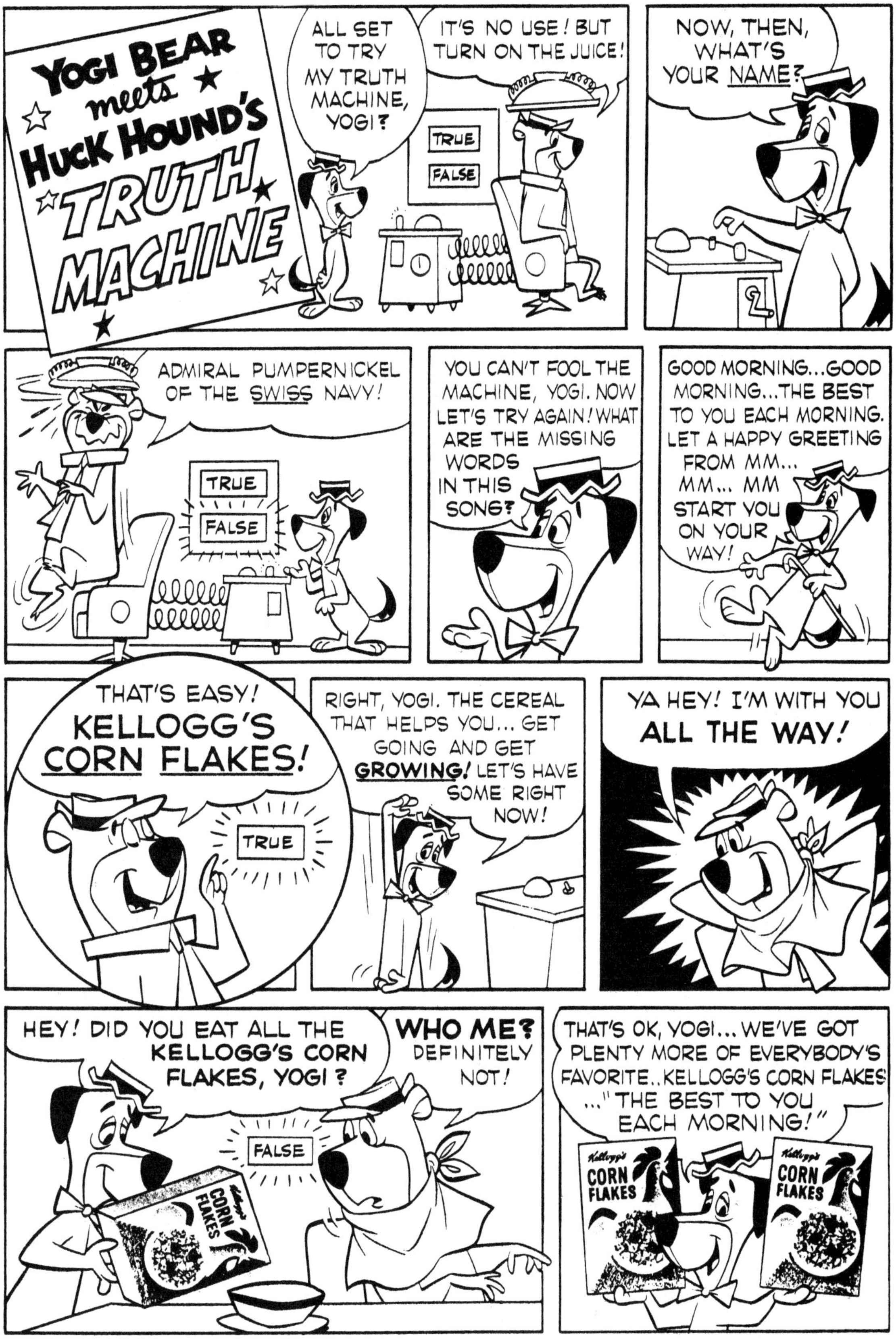
YOGI BEAR meets HUCK HOUND'S TRUTH MACHINE
ALL SET TO TRY MY TRUTH MACHINE, YOGI?
IT'S NO USE! BUT TURN ON THE JUICE!
TRUE
FALSE
NOW, THEN, WHAT'S YOUR NAME?
ADMIRAL PUMPERNICKEL OF THE SWISS NAVY!
TRUE
FALSE
YOU CAN'T FOOL THE MACHINE, YOGI. NOW LET'S TRY AGAIN! WHAT ARE THE MISSING WORDS IN THIS SONG?
GOOD MORNING...GOOD MORNING...THE BEST TO YOU EACH MORNING. LET A HAPPY GREETING FROM MM... MM... MM START YOU ON YOUR WAY!
THAT'S EASY! KELLOGG'S CORN FLAKES!
TRUE
RIGHT, YOGI. THE CEREAL THAT HELPS YOU... GET GOING AND GET GROWING! LET'S HAVE SOME RIGHT NOW!
YA HEY! I'M WITH YOU ALL THE WAY!
HEY! DID YOU EAT ALL THE KELLOGG'S CORN FLAKES, YOGI?
WHO ME? DEFINITELY NOT!
FALSE
Kellogg's CORN FLAKES
THAT'S OK, YOGI... WE'VE GOT PLENTY MORE OF EVERYBODY'S FAVORITE..KELLOGG'S CORN FLAKES! ..."THE BEST TO YOU EACH MORNING!"
Kellogg's CORN FLAKES
Kellogg's CORN FLAKES

gathered up not only the H-B characters, but the Kellogg's animated characters as well. Huck and the gang even did their own commercials for Kellogg's putting characters like Cornelius the Rooster, who appeared on the box of Corn Flakes, into an early retirement.

Some of the H-B characters even appeared on the front of boxes, most notably Yogi Bear (a regular on OK's), Snagglepuss (a favorite on Cocoa Krispies) and Quick Draw McGraw. "Kellogg's is so pleased with the afternoon series that

Below:
Cap'n Crunch stars in this comic book give away from the '80s.
©1991 Quaker

store displays and billboards across the country feature Hanna-Barbera characters and five million boxes of cereal a day come out of the plant with full-size pictures of Yogi or Jinks or Huck," declared a magazine article in 1961. (An interesting sidenote is that while modern audiences know Fred Flintstone and Barney Rubble as the shills for Pebbles cereals, they started their commercial career advertising Winston cigarettes.)

Other cereal companies followed suit and began to develop identifiable characters, in particular General Mills. One of the first of their successes was the Trix Rabbit who hated carrots and went crazy for the "fruit flavors" of Trix cereal. "Silly Rabbit, Trix are for kids" was his constant reminder when his series of disguises failed to help him reach his goal. Since the Fifties (and originally in black and white so audiences didn't see those wonderful fruit colors), the likable rabbit tried hard but unsuccessfully for a taste.

General Mills realized audiences were becoming as frustrated as the rabbit, so during the 1976 presidential elections, they ran an extremely popular advertising campaign where people could determine whether the rabbit should be given a bowl of Trix. Over 99% of the box top ballots

sided with the rabbit who got his taste of Trix but when he asked for more, he was told to wait until the next election. Now, almost 15 years later, the rabbit will finally get another bowl of Trix with the new lime green flavor when he wins the bicycle race known as the Tour De Trix.

Another crazed character from General Mills was Sonny the Cuckoo Bird who went "Cuckoo for Cocoa Puffs." In the beginning he was teamed with an older cuckoo named Gramps who continually tormented Sonny by showing him the cereal. However audiences who were surveyed felt the Gramps character was too "mean" so he disappeared, to be replaced with a string of children to continually torment Sonny. (It seems odd in this era of "just say 'no,'" that such humor about addictions, even to a cereal, is permitted by those who police children's programming.)

In addition, General Mills was responsible for introducing to the world of the Seventies Frankenberry, Count Chocula, Booberry the ghost, and Fruit Brute the werewolf who, despite being suggestive of the classic Universal Studios monsters, were actually cowards who staunchly argued the merits of their namesake cereals. (Not long ago there was some controversy over a box of Count Chocula featuring an illustration of Bela Lugosi's Dracula. It seemed the original Count was wearing a five-pointed star, which many deemed resembled the Jewish Star of David. The box featuring this artwork was quickly withdrawn.)

General Mills needed a sense of humor when they sponsored Jay Ward's *Rocky And His Friends* because Ward and crew turned right around and devised a Rocky and Bullwinkle serial story poking fun at box top collecting with Boris Badenov counterfeiting the precious box tops and ruining the economy. Bullwinkle ended up the spokesmoose for Cheerios anyway, sharing those honors with the Cheerios Kid ("Go-Go-Power with Cheerios").

In 1963, Quaker cereals entered the field in a big way. They had Jay Ward and crew develop one of the most popular cereal salesmen, Cap'n Crunch, even before the cereal existed. The TV promotion was carefully planned and helped Cap'n Crunch become the most popular new cereal of the decade. Using his own staff of writers, animators and voice artists, Ward created mini-masterpieces that reflected his own unique sense of humor as well as selling a product.

The skipper of the S.S. Guppy had a group of

children and the ever-faithful Seadog help him obtain or guard the cereal from such foes as Jean La Foote, the barefoot pirate. New characters, like the Crunch Bird (from the island of Crunchberries) and Smedly the elephant representing Peanut Butter Crunch cereal, often popped up as well.

"You know the Cap'n Crunch commercials? The good ship Guppy, and the crew and the adventures and the pirates and the strange creatures and so forth?...that world was invented by Allan Burns, who was at that time a writer for Jay Ward. Allan Burns later took the same expertise and invented *The Mary Tyler Moore Show* and *Lou Grant*," said producer Bill Scott at a lecture at UCLA in 1983.

Above: Animation drawing of Quake. ©1991 Quaker

Ward's team was also responsible for Quisp and Quake, who in the mid-Sixties were involved in a somewhat friendly rivalry about who had the better cereal. The powerful miner Quake, whose cereal came from the center of the earth, was later softened into a less imposing super-hero-costumed Australian cowboy and was constantly being teased by a small propeller topped spaceman named Quisp who looked remarkably like an improved design of the moon men from the *Rocky And His Friends* show.

Animated commercials are also subject to network restrictions concerning violence, which began in the late Sixties. Bill Scott complained, "We've had to remove the Captain's sword.

He can't even brandish it anymore."

Even though Kellogg's and General Mills were the unquestioned leaders in the use of animated characters to sell cereal, Post cereals was responsible for a unique achievement—an entire Saturday morning cartoon show featuring its own animated heroes. When the *Linus The Lionhearted* show premiered on CBS in September 1964, audiences were already familiar with the characters from earlier cereal commercials. Linus the lion had proclaimed the benefits of Crispy Critters ("the one and only cereal that comes in the shape of animals"), while postman, Lovable Truly, was a natural for promoting the cereal of "letters," Alpha-Bits and a very early version of Sugar Bear (before he was fully a vocal imitation of Bing Crosby) hawked Sugar Crisp. Joined by another Post spokesperson, so-Hi (featured on Rice Krinkles), they were voiced by some of the top vocal talent of the day including Sheldon Leonard, Carl Reiner, Jonathan Winters and Sterling Holloway.

Under today's restrictions, such a show would be inconceivable since at the time it was, in fact, a half hour long commercial for Post cereals, even though the individual segments never mentioned the product and audiences viewing the

Above: Linus the Lion-hearted from Post's Crispy Critters: "the one and only cereal that comes in the shape of animals." ©1991 Post

episodes today might not make the product connection. The character of the bewildered monarch, Linus, was so appealing that he appeared in his own comic book from Gold Key and as a balloon in the Macy's Thanksgiving Day Parade. The show, itself, continued to be rerun on Saturday morning until 1969.

It was not just Linus who was merchandised. Animated cereal characters popped up everywhere from a "Kellogg's Frosted Flakes" lunchbox from Aladdin with a smiling Tony the Tiger to a

wind-up Trix cereal alarm clock with the crazy rabbit's face to a vinyl squeaker figurine set of Snap, Crackle and Pop. Many of these collectible items could only be purchased with boxtops (or, now, proof of purchase seals) or found inside the boxes, but some were sold in actual stores alongside similar merchandise of theatrical and television characters.

Today, companies are more aware than ever of the merchandising potential of their properties. Many of the characters and personalities used to sell cereal (and other products) are being exploited on merchandise sold in stores across the country and the world.

This cross-over worked the other way at times with cereals being created based on animated properties. The Pink Panther, the Smurfs, Mighty Mouse, the Jetsons, Popeye, the Teenage Mutant Ninja Turtles and Warners' Tiny Toon Adventures are just some of the characters that have had cereals developed to showcase them. Obviously these animated breakfast grains were promoted via animated commercials.

Cereals, of course, were not the only commercials to use animated characters. Many memorable characters like the Frito Bandito (retired in his prime amidst cries of racism), the Hamm's Bear (revived and revised over and over again because his familiarity quotient is so high) and Charlie Tuna ("Sorry, Charlie!") entertained audiences and more importantly burned name brand recognition into the minds of consumers. Most of these mini movies are produced by numerous studios who specialize in commercials.

However the bigger name studios were originally involved. Hanna-Barbera, whose earliest shows were sponsored by Kellogg's, did most of the commercials for the sponsors. Even Disney got on the band wagon in the Fifties and Sixties supplying animated commercials for Peter Pan Peanut Butter (which featured Tinkerbell) and 7-Up (starring Freddie, a bird) among other products.

Disney's version of Winnie the Pooh even became box featured for Nabisco's Wheat Honeys and Rice Honeys cereals in the Sixties. (Earlier, Buffalo Bee hawked the honey flavored cereal and even appeared in his own comic book.)

Often times popular animated characters were transformed into breakfast cereals like Mighty Mouse, Popeye, Flintstones, Teenage Mutant Ninja Turtles, the Pink Panther, the Smurfs and many others. The bond between animated personalities and cereal is a tradition that continues today especially since the younger set is still a major focus for breakfast cereal sales.

Today, cereal is part of a balanced breakfast. There is

Above:
Nabisco's Buffalo Bee, in his own comic book, with his girl friend, Honey Bee, from 1959.
©1959 National Biscuit Company

Left:
Drawing from the Trix Rabbit's model sheets.

a growing interest in adult cereals, and more nutrition in general. This trend is mostly affecting the names of cereals. The "sugar" has gone out of many brands including Sugar Frosted Flakes (now just Frosted Flakes), Sugar Crisp (now Golden Crisp), Sugar Pops (now Corn Pops) and even Sugar Smacks (now Honey Smacks).

One cereal to jump on this adult approach was General Mills' Honey Nut Cheerios. The animated protagonist is a bee who continually interrupts people doing worthwhile projects like reading, playing outside, or working puzzles. He wants the person to stop what they're doing and have a bowl of the sweetened Cheerios. (Regular Cheerios advertise that regular Cheerios have less sugar than most cereals.) This series of commercials has taken several amusing turns, including having the bee interrupt Warner Brothers famed Wile E. Coyote trying to get the Road Runner. In the end, Wile E. prefers Honey Nut Cheerios to the Road Runner. (Other animated stars "guesting" in commercials included Popeye joining Sonny for Cocoa Puffs and Bugs Bunny working with the Trix Rabbit.)

The desire to create new characters continues on,

Below right: Babs and Buster Bunny (no relation), and their Tiny Toon Adventures series, are some of the latest cartoon stars to be the basis of a cereal. ©1991 Quaker/ ©1991 and ™ Warner Brothers

Below: Pink Panther Flakes featured frosted corn flakes colored pink. ©1991 Post/ DePatie-Freleng

though not always successfully. In recent years there have been attempts to create many new heroes including Kellogg's O.J. (for OJ's, a cereal with orange juice in it), General Mills' Ice Cream Jones (for Ice Cream Cones Cereal) and Yummy Mummy (for Fruity Yummy Mummy). One new popular character is Bigg Mixx (for Bigg Mixx) a strange creature consisting of part moose, part chicken, part pig, etc.

As if to bring the entire business back to basics, Kellogg's began a new campaign in 1991 for Corn Flakes. It features the Kellogg's Rooster (still referred to as Cornelius) jumping out of the box and trying to crow. This is the start to a new series of commercials that will feature the character in animated commercials. Far different from the "funny animal" look of the Fifties and Sixties' Hanna-Barbera version, this Nineties' Rooster is sleek and stylistic in design. The original cereal, from the original company, once again jumps on the cartoon bandwagon. It really is a good morning.

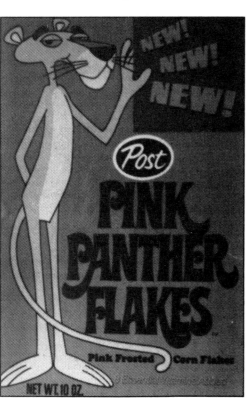

TOP SECRET
CHAPTER FIVE:

THE ANIMATED ADVENTURES OF DICK TRACY

Dick Tracy has been shot, tortured, stabbed, and maimed many times. Regrettably, he didn't fare much better in the world of animation. For over half a century, while he achieved success in a variety of media, animation fame eluded him. In all the books that have been written about the character, there is always a missing chapter about

*Below:
Daffy Duck as
Duck Twacy.
© Warner
Brothers*

America's most famous detective's adventures in animation.

Dick Tracy was the first of what was considered a realistic police strip. From its first appearance in October 1931, it was a brutal and violent adventure strip populated by some of the most outrageous villains of all time. It was also one of the most successful strips of

all time and continues to appear in newspapers today almost 60 years after its creation.

In the early days of animation, many funny comic strip characters made the transition to animation. Despite Tracy's cartoony villains and the exaggerated face of Tracy himself, Dick Tracy was considered a serious adventure strip and

"The Great Piggy Bank Robbery"

A Looney Tune CARTOON in TECHNICOLOR

A WARNER BROS. CARTOON

that type of property was not generally developed for the early animated cartoons.

In the Thirties and Forties, it was the inspiration for a series of movie serials and feature films, most of them starring Ralph Byrd as the famous detective. Also in the Forties, a popular radio program chronicled the further adventures of the hook-nosed policeman. In the early Fifties, there was a short lived TV series which also starred Ralph Byrd.

The Sixties had producer William Dozier, following the success of his Batman TV show, film a pilot for a Dick Tracy series. He experimented with latex makeup for the villains although none of the classic villains appeared in the finished pilot. (Dozier used actor Victor Buono as a computer whiz to give Tracy a run for his money.) The Disney feature film was almost a decade in the making as studio after studio considered, developed and eventually dropped the film.

However, the cinematic and TV history of Dick Tracy is not without its cartoon side. Dick Tracy has made occasional forays into the world of animated films, including his own series in 1960.

So well known a character was Dick Tracy that in 1942's *Dumb Hounded* (MGM), the debut of Tex Avery's Droopy, Droopy is seen reading a Dick Tracy comic book to pick up tricks of the trade. Dick Tracy makes a larger "appearance" (in a way) in Warners' *The Great Piggy Bank Robbery* (1946). This Daffy Duck cartoon is a favorite of many animation and comic fans. Written by Warren Foster and directed by Bob Clampett, it parodies the world of Dick Tracy.

One morning in the barnyard, Daffy Duck is even more frantic than usual. He is awaiting the arrival of the mailman in the hopes that he will bring the latest comic book issue of the adventures of Dick Tracy. Daffy's patience is rewarded and the issue arrives in his mailbox. "I can hardly wait to see what happens to Dick Tracy! I love that man!" sputters the little black duck.

Accidentally knocking himself out while reading the comic book, Daffy imagines himself as the famous "de-teck-it-tive," Duck Twacy. Duck Twacy starts receiving a flood of calls from people who have had their piggy banks stolen. He is relatively unconcerned until he discovers that his own piggy bank is missing and with a huge magnifying glass immediately takes to the street to search for clues. At one point he bumps into Sherlock Holmes and tells the Baker Street detective to get lost because Duck Twacy is "workin'" this side of the street."

He eventually takes a street car to the criminals' hideout, which is clearly marked by signs and banners. It is a trap and he falls through a trap door. Following footprints, he even walks along the ceiling, remarking to the audience, "Nothing's impossible to Duck Twacy!"

He quickly realizes that the piggy bank robbery was the work of some of Duck Twacy's greatest enemies. These characters were parodies of the Chester Gould method of creating ugly, outrageous crooks with outlandish names. Twacy's rogue's gallery includes Mouse Man, Snake Eyes, 88-Teeth, Hammer Head, Pussycat Puss, Juke Box Jaw and Wolf Man. The villains chase the duck.

At this point, one of Gould's most famous criminal creations makes a cameo appearance. Flattop stands expressionless as tiny planes take off from the top of his head. Flattop was also the term used for a navy ship with a flat deck where planes took off and landed at sea. It was a type of pun immediately recognized by audiences in the Forties and it was the type of word play that showed up in a lot of Bob Clampett cartoons.

After turning Pumpkin Head into a stack of pumpkin pies and Neon Noodle into a neon sign that flashes "Eat At Joe's," Duck Twacy traps the other crooks in a closet and very violently uses a machine gun to pepper the door with a hail of bullets. Upon opening the door, the dead crooks, now filled with bullet holes, tumble to the floor one by one. It was a moment Gould must have loved as the bad guys got their just desserts in a violent and cruel climax.

As the last villain tumbles to the floor, Duck Twacy discovers the missing piggy banks. Locating his own, he passionately kisses the bank. Naturally, during this action, he awakes to discover himself kissing a fat pig in the pig sty! (Later a children's storytelling record set was released that featured a story written by Warren Foster and illustrated by Bob McKimson where Daffy Duck once again became Duck Twacy.)

It wasn't until the early Sixties that Tracy was finally allowed to star in his own cartoons. UPA, the studio that had created such characters as Mr. Magoo and Gerald McBoing Boing, was having financial

Right:
UPA's Dick Tracy.
© 1991 UPA

Above:
UPA introduced Joe Jitsu
© 1991 UPA

problems and decided to move into TV production. They produced over a hundred Magoo episodes for TV. At the same time, the company produced almost an equal number of episodes for a show entitled *The Adventures Of Dick Tracy* (later retitled *The Dick Tracy Show*).

Premiering in 1961, the show had well-known radio and stage performer Everett Sloane as the voice of Dick Tracy. Sloane is perhaps best remembered for his important roles in Orson Welles' films like *Citizen Kane* and *Lady From Shanghai*.

The stories were contributed by a host of good storymen who had impressive credentials from working at studios like Disney and Lantz. Those storymen included Homer Brightman, Al Bertino, Dick Kinney, Ralph Wright, Bob

Ogle, Dick Shaw, Ed Nofzinger and more. Supervising director was Abe Levitow who oversaw the work of Brad Case, Clyde Geronimi, Ray Patterson and others who directed individual segments. Unfortunately, with so many stories being turned out so quickly and the thrust of the show being aimed at young children, these storymen were locked into a restrictive formula that didn't allow them an opportunity to showcase America's most famous detective.

In each half hour show, there were usually four short adventures and several Crimestopper Tips. The Crimestopper Tips, borrowed from a concept Gould had used on his Sunday Dick Tracy page, featured Dick Tracy giving the viewers information on how to stop crimes. On the animated show, these tips ranged from not touching anything in a room that has been burglarized until the police took fingerprints to being cautious about salesmen with bargains because the goods might be stolen. The Crimestopper Tips were also used in true Gould fashion to promote the police department and how it was a fine career that would give a young man a chance at public service along with job security.

Each half hour show opened with a speeding police car careening down crowded streets and finally coming to a stop in front of Police Station E. The beginning of each individual segment had Dick Tracy sitting behind his desk, apparently just having received important crime information from his Chief. Tracy would immediately talk into his wrist radio, being careful to lift his arm to obscure his mouth so that animators would not have to animate the lips moving, and assign the case to one of four different officers who worked for him.

Those four characters were Hemlock Holmes with the Retouchables, Jo Jitsu (also spelled Joe Jitsu on occasion), Go Go Gomez and Heap O'Calory. These characters were in the animation tradition of extreme ethnic stereotypes, except for Hemlock Holmes who might be described as a

funny animal.

Hemlock Holmes was a bull dog with an old fashioned tall policeman's helmet with a big star on it. He talked like a bad imitation of Cary Grant. Holmes supervised a group of policemen known as the Retouchables who seemed to be inspired by the classic silent slapstick comedy group, the Keystone Cops. Obviously, Holmes' name was meant to parody the name of Sherlock Holmes while the Retouchables was a parody name of The Untouchables, the famous gangster fighting group led by Elliot Ness and the basis for a popular television show familiar to viewers when the animated series debuted. A typical adventure was "The Catnip Caper" where these foul-ups had to stop Stooge Viller and Mumbles from kidnapping a famous cat from a cat show at the Hotel Ritz.

Heap O'Calory was a good natured, red-haired foot patrolman who was quite overweight and talked like actor Andy Devine. He only lacked an Irish accent to resemble the typical bumbling policeman popular in films of the Forties. A typical adventure was "Penny Ante Caper" where he must stop Pruneface and Itchyfrom stealing pennies from Penny Arcades. Like Hemlock Holmes, Heap generally captured the crooks by accident at the last

Above: Tracy conveniently holds his wrist radio over his lips so animators won't need to animate his mouth.
© 1991 UPA

moment before Dick Tracy would arrive.

Jo Jitsu was the smartest and perhaps most effective of Tracy 's crew. He was clearly an Oriental stereotype. He was short, wore huge thick glasses, and spoke with a strong Japanese accent when he gave "fortune cookie" type dialog. Naturally, he was a master of Karate and Ju Jitsu (the martial art from which he derived his name). Jo's bowler hat hid a rather severe haircut that was reminiscent of the World War II cartoons of Japanese soldiers. Jo's calm detecting skill and wisecracks were meant to suggest to the audience other similar Oriental detectives like Charlie Chan or Mr. Moto. A typical adventure was "The Newspaper Caper" where Pruneface and Itchy attempt to blow up a newspaper plant. (This segment offered an interesting resolution and the resolution to the episode. The crooks have been run

The Animated Adventures Of Dick Tracy

through the newspaper press by Jo, and appear in a Dick Tracy Sunday funnies page with Jo and Tracy!)

Like Jo, Go Go Gomez did not wear a police uniform. He was attired in sandals, a white Mexican peasant outfit and a big white sombrero. Also, like Jo, Go Go usually captured the crooks by using his brains rather than by accident. Go Go loved disguising himself and annoying the crooks to distraction. Supposedly, some of the humor was based on the fact that Go Go was always taking a siesta at the beginning of his segments and was a typical lazy stereotype but when called into action by Tracy, he could really "go go" as fast as Speedy Gonzales. A typical adventure was "Court Jester" where Stooge Viller and Mumbles are on trial for forgery and Stooge escapes so Go Go must track him down and return him to court.

In most segments, each of these officers would confront a pair from Tracy's classic rogue gallery: Sketch Paree was teamed with The Mole, Pruneface with Itchy, Flattop with B. B. Eyes, Stooge Viller with Mumbles and the Brow with Oodles. Familiar voice artists like Paul Frees, June Foray and Jerry Hausner supplied voices for the characters. Mel Blanc's name appears in books and on video boxes as a voice performer on the show but reportedly only voiced the Go Go Gomez character on a "pilot" episode for the series and Paul Frees took over the vocal chores for that character for the rest of the series.

To remind audiences that this was in fact *The Dick Tracy Show,* the famous detective generally only made two other appearances in each segment besides his initial assigning of the case. In the middle of a deadly threat like a falling piano about to behead Hemlock or a car about to run over Jo Jitsu, the characters would shout "Hold Everything! " All action would freeze while the character contacted Dick Tracy to let him know how the case was progressing. As soon as they

finished talking with Tracy, the action would resume. Tracy also appeared at the very end of each segment to say "Good work, Hemlock, " or "Nice Going, Heap, " when he saw that they had captured the bad guys who were often battered into insensibility at that point. There were rare exceptions where Tracy did appear more actively involved in the storyline.

The show was popular enough to spark some merchandising tied in directly to the show and not just solely to Dick Tracy. Ideal Toy Company released in 1961 a series of three hand puppets, each boxed separately, of Dick Tracy, Hemlock Holmes and Jo Jitsu. Each box also contained "an unbreakable record featuring TV voices" of the three characters. A Kenner Sparkle Paint set offered pictures of Tracy, Jo Jitsu, Go Go Gomez and Flattop and Mumbles. *Dick Tracy,* a Little Golden Book published in 1962, featured Dick and the animated

characters like Jo Jitsu. (Jo was perhaps the most popular of the crew and also appeared with Tracy on an autographed card that came with the "Crimestopper Club" kit issued in the early Sixties by the Chicago Tribune.)

After its initial syndicated run, *The Dick Tracy Show* appeared sporadically on local television stations over the

*Above:
Itchy, The Mole,
and Flat Top.
©1991 UPA*

years. However, in June 1990, the cartoons were re-released to coincide with the release of Disney's live action feature *Dick Tracy* starring Warren Beatty. The animated show scored some impressive ratings but also sparked outraged protests from Asian and Latino groups upset over the portrayals of Jo Jitsu and Go Go Gomez. In the Los Angeles area, where the

"Okay, Chief. I'll get on it right away."

Above: Flyer for the release to home video of the UPA Cartoons. ©1991 UPA

cartoons were running on the Disney owned independent station KCAL (Channel 9), the minority groups were particularly vocal.

"When you exaggerate racial and ethnic mannerisms and characteristics, that is racism, no matter how you slice it," said Raul Ruiz, Chicano studies professor at Cal State Northridge. "It should have been obvious that the show was offensive."

Ron Wakabayashi, executive director of the Los Angeles City Human Relations Commission and a member of the Japanese American Citizens League commented that, "You don't see caricatures today in that overt form. I would only hope Disney would view it as surprising and appalling. Because you're focusing on a young audience, there's the likelihood that kids may transfer these names and impressions toward minority kids they know."

On July 16, 1990, president of UPA, Henry Saperstein responded to the criticisms in a guest editorial in the Los Angeles Times. "With extreme characters like Pruneface, The Brow, Mumbles, Itchy, and the Mole in a *Dick Tracy* cartoon would you do Go Go and Joe as whitebread WASPs?...The *Tracy* cartoons portray Go Go and Joe as good clean cops who don't take bribes or get indicted, and consistently bring criminals to justice. How about focusing on these attributes as 'role models' instead of exaggerating a nothing controversy from a self-appointed tiny do-gooder protest group?...C'mon guys, these are only cartoons--sit back and enjoy them."

The cartoons were removed from KCAL and other stations but at the same time Paramount Home Video released six volumes under the title *The Animated Adventures of Dick Tracy* to stores. Some stations returned the cartoons to the air when UPA re-edited the series to eliminate the Jo Jitsu and Go Go Gomez segments.

For fans who wanted to see the famous cop in action, this animated show was a disappointment. Ironically, Chester Gould was an advisor on the series. When he was interviewed in the early Seventies, he was asked about his feelings about the show.

"I didn't like that," he grumbled, "That was made on a format I came up with and supervised the initial episode. But we were catering to very small fry and I think we would have been smarter to have taken a more serious view of the thing and played it more or less straight, like the strip."

Actually, UPA did finally do a straight half hour Dick Tracy adventure, "Dick Tracy and The Mob." This long forgotten half hour was part of *The Famous Adventures Of Mr. Magoo* series. Thanks to the success of the animated Christmas special, *Mr. Magoo's Christmas Carol* (1960), the character of Mr. Magoo was revived for a prime time network series call *The Famous Adventures Of Mr. Magoo* (1964). Following the format of the Christmas special, Magoo was cast in the roles of famous literary characters. Magoo appeared in such diverse parts as Dr. Frankenstein, Don Quixote, Rip Van Winkle and Dr. Watson among others. Magoo really was out of character with none of the elements that made him a cartoon favorite. However, "Dick Tracy and the Mob" proved a unique episode in the series as Magoo played the part of...Mr. Magoo.

"Dick Tracy and the Mob" opened with Dick Tracy and his men, disguised as street workers. They foil an armored car robbery by Flattop and Itchy and there is an actual gun battle in the street with people getting wounded or killed. The crooks escape to Pruneface's mansion which is surrounded by an electric fence and vicious dogs. At the mansion, Pruneface is the chairman of the board of a group of crooks including Flattop, Itchy, The Mole, Mumbles and The Brow. Upset that Tracy has been interfering with their criminal activities, Pruneface has made arrangements with

a top hit man, named Squinty Eyes, to kill Tracy.

Back at headquarters, the Chief gets a tip from Interpol that the American mobster Squinty Eyes is heading for the States. Squinty Eyes was suspected of many killings and has been out of the country for ten years. He looks just like Mr. Magoo except he has a Moe Howard haircut and smokes a big cigar. (Actually the f ile on Squinty Eyes has the inside joke: "Voice: Sounds very much like Jim Backus. " Backus was the voice of Mr. Magoo.)

As luck would have it, Tracy passes by a theater where Mr . Magoo is performing in "The Famous Adventures of Mr. Magoo, " a one-man stage show in its 26th week. Impressed by the performance, and the resemblance of Magoo to the

crook, Tracy goes backstage after the show.

"Mr. Magoo, my name is Tracy. Dick Tracy. Police Lieutenant," says Tracy. "If it's about that traffic ticket, I paid it last week," replies Magoo. Tracy convinces Magoo to impersonate Squinty Eyes, "the most important, the most dramatic role of your career."

Tracy, disguised as a cab driver, picks up Squinty Eyes at the airport and transports him directly to police headquarters. Magoo has been hiding in the front seat, listening, so that he can imitate Squinty Eyes' voice. While the mobster is being kept in custody, Magoo disguises himself as the crook and keeps the appointment at Pruneface's place. The police want to discover why the mob has sent for a hit man.

Magoo is told he has to kill Dick Tracy. Flattop is sent along to make sure the job gets done. Magoo has to wire explosives to Tracy's car so it will explode. Fortunately, since he was unable to contact Tracy ahead of time, he leaves a note in the car so that while the car blows up, Tracy survives. Flattop, however, doesn't see the detective escape at the last minute and on their return to the mansion, tells the mob that Tracy is dead.

Unfortunately, Pruneface's contacts have let him know that Tracy is still

Left:
Tracy's second appearance in a UPA series, this time starring Mr. Magoo.
©1991 UPA

The Animated Adventures Of Dick Tracy

alive. During this activity, the real Squinty Eyes has escaped and naturally heads for Pruneface's place. Tracy and the police are close behind, hoping to arrive in time to save Magoo.

Magoo literally loses his hair, revealing himself to be a police spy, when the real Squinty Eyes shows up. Magoo is bound and gagged and left in the room with sticks of dynamite ready to explode when Tracy and the police enter the room . The crooks escape in a helicopter. Magoo manages to get off his chair although he is still tied up by rope. He edges his way across the floor like a worm and is able to kick the dynamite out the window just as Tracy arrives and the dynamite explodes .

Magoo's one

disappointment is that he will be unable to get any publicity for his help. If the mob found out who it was who fooled them, Magoo's life wouldn't be worth a plugged nickel. Tracy explains this to the poor actor. "My public will never hear of the greatest performance of my career," Magoo moans, "But perhaps there will be other occasions when my talent is needed."

Unfortunately, Tracy never called again which was a shame because this episode, despite Mr. Magoo, did capture some of the flair of Gould's comic strip. It didn't suggest the darkness of Gould's world, but it did present a good characterization of the straight shooting Dick Tracy and despite the handicap of a limited budget, did feature some fast moving action and a simple, but well told, story. This atypical episode was written by Sloan Nibley. Abe Levitow was supervising director. Ray Patterson was sequence director and Grant Simmons was animation director. Voices were supplied by Marvin Miller, Howard Morris, Dennis King, Jr. and Shep Menkin.

Dick Tracy returned again to the animated world of TV in 1971. *Archie's TV Funnies* (1971) was another of the many variations of Filmation's *The Archie Show* that had begun in 1968 and would last until 1978. The Archie characters were the

popular Riverdale High School teens: Archie, Reggie, Jughead, Betty and Veronica. The concept behind *Archie's TV Funnies* was that the gang was producing a TV show that featured their favorite cartoon characters.

Each half hour had a framing story involving The Archies but was primarily composed of short, individual cartoon segments featuring cartoon characters from the following group: "The Dropouts," "Moon Mullins," "Smokey Stover," "Nancy & Sluggo," "Emmy Lou, " "The Captain and the Kids, " "Alley Oop," "Broom Hilda" and "Dick Tracy."

An example of a typical Dick Tracy adventure in the series was about a bank robbery in which the crooks were protected from the police by trained dogs. Pruneface had stolen the dogs from all over the city to train them to be "anti-police" dogs. The Chief calls upon Tracy to help. The whole cast of characters listen to the problem including Tess Trueheart (not yet Dick's wife), Junior Tracy, Moonmaid and Sam Catchem. They have to find and destroy the operation.

Pruneface has fooled a very rich Miss Canine into letting him and his men use her mansion as the "retraining" area for the dogs for his international crime syndicate. Tracy uses a radio controlled robot dog, Rookie, as bait. Pruneface's men steal the dog. Using the TV cameras in Rookie's eyes and their magnetic air cars, Tracy and Sam locate the mansion. However, Tess, following her own lead, has shown up at the mansion at the same time .

Recognizing her as Tracy's friend, Pruneface ties up Tess and Miss Canine in the basement and then the crooks head for the border in their van. As she tries to escape, Tess breaks a water pipe and the locked basement quickly fills with water. Tess and Miss Canine seem doomed to a death by drowning. However, the TV transmitter in Rookie's eyes has not been deactivated and Tracy sees the danger.

Tracy rescues the ladies and then rejoins Sam. To prevent the crooks from escaping, Dick in his magnetic air car uses his rifle (actually a "Telescopic Laser Projector") to open the bridge just as the van crosses, trapping the van in the half-open bridge.

Back at headquarters, Tracy asks Tess if she's learned her lesson to stay out of police work. Tess says she has but a report about Flattop escaping prison gives her new inspiration and the episode ends with her telling Dick that she knows exactly what to do.

Archie's TV Funnies was directed by Hal Sutherland and written by Jim Ryan, Bill Danch and Ken Sobol. Voices were supplied by Howard

Morris, John Erwin, Dallas McKennon and Jane Webb. The Dick Tracy segment was obviously a selling point because each half hour opened with Archie Andrews smiling at the audience and picking up the Sunday paper and the first

Above: Disney's "Mick Tracy" was used for corporate merchandise. ©1991 Walt Disney Company

comic strip he saw had the Dick Tracy logo, followed by the famous profile filling the TV screen. However, when Filmation did a similar series in 1978 entitled *The Fabulous Funnies* featuring some of these same cartoon characters, Dick Tracy was no longer along for the ride.

Despite what at least one animation book states, these were not repeats of the UPA cartoons but new cartoons. More so than any other animated version so far of Tracy, this version tried to keep closely to the basic Tracy lore. Tracy's famous yellow raincoat, absent in the other versions, made the character stand out.

That same year (1971), after the completion of the X-rated, animated feature *Fritz The Cat*, Ralph Bakshi and Steve Krantz announced that they were in the process of developing *Dick Tracy: Frozen, Fried And Buried Alive*. It was to be set in Chicago during the depression and as the title suggested, Tracy would be in the type of jeopardy that was a key element of his early adventures. The newspapers reported that creator Chester Gould would be paid more than $100,000

for the animation rights.

Unfortunately, the partnership of Bakshi and Krantz broke up soon after the announcement and it became just another of the many Bakshi announced animated projects that never saw completion.

Although known for its strong animation, Disney followed a long standing tradition of seeking to transfer the famous comic strip detective to the live action screen instead of an animated feature. An interesting sidenote is that this is not the first time Tracy has encountered the Disney organization. On January, 6, 1982, the comic strip episode of the Dick Tracy daily strip had Dick and his family at Disneyland. Although the famous park wasn't mentioned by name, the strip had a drawing of the famous Sleeping Beauty castle and Dick's son, Joe, was talking with a Br'er Bear costumed

character. During this story sequence, Dick and crew were supposed to be in the Southern California area so that left little doubt that they were at "the Happiest Place on Earth."

After Disney's *Dick Tracy* came out, an imaginative Disney artist redesigned the distinctive face logo so that the shadowy profile now resembled Mickey Mouse and was dubbed "Mick Tracy." The design was so popular that a limited amount of merchandise, available only to Disney employees, was released.

Many of the elements that have helped make Dick Tracy so popular for over half a century could inspire a truly memorable animated film. Until then, his animated career will merely be another interesting footnote in this flatfoot's long and colorful history.

TOP SECRET
CHAPTER SIX:

TOONS ON THE AIR:
RADIO TOONS

Toons On The Air: Radio Toons

Tuning around the radio dial today, it is more than likely that the air will be filled with the sounds of a Top Forty station playing the latest musical hits or an intense talk show with people debating the newest topic of interest. For most of the first half of this century, though, radio was equal to motion pictures as a key source of entertainment; it was a home to countless comedy, variety, quiz and dramatic shows.

Like such TV series as *The Simpsons, Twin Peaks* or *L.A. Law* radio had people planning their lives around their favorite programs. Folks stayed home certain nights so that they wouldn't miss the newest episode of *Lum And Abner, The Edgar Bergen And Charlie McCarthy Show, The Jack Benny Show, Amos 'N' Andy, The Shadow* and others. These shows were bound to be the center of conversation the next day at the office or at the supermarket.

As with any such popular and influential medium, it created its own language, characters and expressions. Some of these elements became significant additions to popular culture. They were picked up by writers of comics, comic strips, books, movies, and even other radio shows. Similarly, radio borrowed heavily from these other media creating shows based on characters in books, pulp magazines, films and comics.

Above: Radio's Amos 'n' Andy (Charles Correll & Freeman Gosden) turned to animation, creating Calvin and the Colonel. © Kayro Productions

The makers of theatrical cartoons of the time were equally involved in this cross pollination.

When TV finally came on the scene, radio series began to fade. Many of the popular shows tried to make the switch to TV, but only a handful really succeeded. The biggest problem was that radio had been a "theatre of the mind." Shows could set their location anywhere their sound effects and music library would allow them. It didn't matter what an actor looked like as long as their voice sounded like the character. Some stars, like Charlie McCarthy, weren't "people" at all, merely a ventriloquist dummy.

This factor kept many shows from being successfully transferred. Adventures and dramas were now restricted to cheap sets and tinny music. Many radio fans were surprised to find their favorite radio character looked nothing at all like the person supplying the voice. Some shows were transformed to TV with a new cast. *Amos 'N' Andy*, performed on radio by a white cast, had to be totally recast with Black actors. Radio wasn't burdened with having to physically create a real world because the listener's mind would do the work.

Animation has a lot in

common with this medium that had to be believed to be seen. Like radio, animation begins with only ideas, writing and voices. With a radio show the listener's mind creates the images. In animation, the storyboard artists, layout crew, animators, background painters and more create the images for the listener, converting the audience into a viewer.

One of the earliest, and most direct, contacts between radio and animation came in 1934 when the Van Beuren studio produced some Amos 'n' Andy cartoons. Using the actual radio stars (and creators of the show), Freeman Gosden (Amos, Kingfish) and Charles Correll (Andy), Van Beuren "visualized" the radio series.

Only two animated shorts were released, but Gosden and Correll made several live action films in black-face as the famed radio stars. Though little remembered today, at the height of Amos 'n' Andy 's popularity it was said a person could walk down a street and not miss a line of the program as it would be playing on every radio in every house on the street! (Gosden and Correll attempted to duplicate their success in the Sixties with *Calvin And The Colonel*. The team produced and voiced this prime time animated series about a bear and a fox

in 1961 which superficially resembled the format of *Amos 'N Andy*. It only lasted one season.)

Animation seldom attempted such a direct conversion of radio to screen again. However, animators

Above: Hollywood has always been a source of animation inspiration. ©1991 Walt Disney Company

were as inspired by the characters and voices on radio as they were by the stars of the cinema. Many cartoon studios used caricatures of popular screen stars as a basis for creating animated characters.

Sometimes these caricatures were just that with the likes of Clark Gable, Jimmy Durante, The Marx Brothers, Laurel and Hardy, Mickey Rooney, Edward G. Robinson and other stars showing up in cartoons from studios like Disney's *Mother Goose Goes To Hollywood* with stars like Katherine Hepburn and W. C. Fields or *Slick Hare* where Humphrey Bogart and Lauren Bacall want Bugs Bunny for dinner and even Terrytoon's *Out Again, In Again* where Heckle and Jeckle disguise themselves as Groucho and Harpo. However, Warners, in particular, seemed to be equally fascinated by the stars of radio.

Below: Warners' Foghorn Leghorn owed much to radio's Senator Claghorn. ©1991 Warner Bros.

In fact, many of the most famous and popular radio comedians of the Thirties and Forties are long forgotten by today's audiences and yet thanks to the Warner cartoons, their personalities and punch lines live on. It is doubtful that today's audience remembers Lew Lehr but his famous trademark line "Monkeys is the cwaziest peepul! " is found in several forms in a number of Warners Cartoons. One example is the finale of Bob Clampett's *Russian Rhapsody* where a Hitler caricature rises from rubble and states "Nutzis is de cwaziest people. "

"Well, now, I wouldn't say that" was originated by Peavey the druggist on *The Great Gildersleeve* radio show. The Mr. Kitzel character on *The Jack Benny Show* was renowned for "It's a possibility!" and "Mmmmm-Could be!" Fred Allen's Mrs. Nussbaum gave "Were you expectink (sic) maybe — (fill in the blank)?" and Titus Moody's "Bub" as in "What's all the hubbub, Bub?" were also well known. Ironically many of these catch phrases still elicit laughs decades later to new generations of audiences who think they originated with Bugs Bunny and Daffy Duck.

Often cartoons were worked around a particularly hot radio talent. Bert Gordon's character, The Mad Russian on *The Eddie Cantor Show* was known for such lines as "Do You min (sic) it?" and "Ho do you do?!" This personality was converted into a Russian dog hunting Bugs Bunny's *Hare Ribbin'*.

Joe Besser, known for his "Not so fa-a-a-a-st!" delivery and his work with the Three Stooges was a popular radio guest star (due to his work with vaudeville greats Olson and Johnson, of *Hellzapoppin'* fame). In *Hollywood Daffy*, his persona was given to the studio guard.

Ed Wynn was another popular comedian of stage and radio. His distinctive voice was appropriated by many cartoon characters including Terrytoon's Gandy

BEAKY BUZZARD

I'M HONGRY!

THESE MEA
IN-A-CAN D
GO VERY F

Goose. Gandy's partner, Sourpuss the Cat, sounded a lot like Jimmy Durante.

Even the dramatic shows gave animation cause for duplication. *Inner Sanctum,* which debuted in 1941, opened with a creaking door and an announcer who stated, "This is Raymond, your host, welcoming you in to the Inner Sanctum." The creaking door and Raymond imitators frequently found their way into animated dialogue and scenes. As did the Shadow's croaky reading of, "Who knows what evil lurks in the hearts of men? The Shadow knows!"

Sometimes an actual series was used as the basis for a short. Chuck Jones' *Hush My Mouse,* a Sniffles cartoon, takes place in Tuffy's Tavern. The locale and characters (except for Sniffles and Edward G. Robincat, a caricature of gangster film king Edward G. Robinson) were all based on the popular *Duffy's Tavern* radio show.

In *Cracked Ice* (1938) W.C. Squeals (a pig version of W.C. Fields) feuds with a member of the theatre audience, an impression of Charlie McCarthy. This was based on Fields and McCarthy's long running radio feud, which found its

way into at least one Fields feature, *You Can't Cheat An Honest Man* (1939). (Fields was the inspiration for one of Warner's last characters, Merlin the Magic Mouse, created in the mid-Sixties.)

One of the most popular comedy shows on radio was *The Jack Benny Show.* Benny was also a popular guest in many Warners shorts. *Daffy Duck And The Dinosaur* (1939) finds Benny as a caveman trying to catch Daffy. *Hollywood Daffy* (1946) finds him trying to win an Oscar from a arcade game. (A running gag on Benny's radio show was how lousy Benny's movies were.) *The Mouse*

Radio Guide 5¢

How to Become a Radio Artist
By Fred Allen

betty boop

By Max Fleischer

MAX FLEISCHER

JANE ALDEN CRASHES RADIO—Now on Magic Voice Program

That Jack Built (1959) features a mouse version of Benny living in Benny's house. All of Benny's cast is in the short from Rochester to Mary Livingston. At the end of the cartoon, it switches to live action and Jack Benny comments on a strange dream.

At this time, it should be stated that many of these characters were not portrayed by the original radio voice; a cartoon voice artist merely copied the voice. Such copying today has gotten a number of advertisers in trouble as more and more courts assert that a person's voice is an identifiable, legally owned

Above: Betty Boop publicizes her radio show. ©1991 King Features

asset.

But in the golden days of radio and animation, little concern was given for such matters. Especially by the courts who failed to find in favor of Helen Kane (whose voice was copied for Betty Boop) and even Mel Blanc (whose famous laugh for Woody Woodpecker was found not to be copyrightable). The studios had almost carte blanc in borrowing "personalities."

The blustering Foghorn Leghorn's voice and personality were almost a direct steal from the character of Senator Beauregard Claghorn performed by Kenny Delmar on *The Fred Allen Show.* In fact, one of Claghorn's familiar catch phrases was "That's a joke, son." Some felt it was no joke when an animated rooster appropriated Delmar's work. In fact, more than one personality at the time felt as if the cartoon voice artists were "stealing" their material and income.

Beaky Buzzard owes a good deal to Edgar Bergen's dumb dummy, Mortimer Snerd. Clampett, a puppet fan, even originally referred to the character as the "Snerd Bird." Tweety, as originally used by Clampett, owes more than a passing nod to Red Skelton's "Mean Widdle Kid."

Sometimes the borrowed voice's owner later moved into animation. Both the

above mentioned Ed Wynn and Joe Besser later did voices for animation. Wynn became the manic Mad Hatter in Disney's *Alice In Wonderland.* Besser began doing voices for Hanna-Barbera TV series including Babu, the genie in *Jeannie* (1973) and Scare Bear in *Yogi's Galaxy Goof-Ups* (1978).

Not all animated voices were borrowed from radio. In some cases, it was an actor's work on radio that brought him to the attention of animators, creating a second (and sometimes bigger) career. Bill Thompson was a popular actor on radio, especially for his role as milquetoast neighbor Wallace Wimple on *Fibber McGee And Molly.* His diminutive voice was picked by Tex Avery to do the original Droopy. Thompson also provided a number of voices for Disney features and shorts including the White Rabbit in *Alice In Wonderland,* Mr. Smee in *Peter Pan* and Audubon J. Woodlore, the park ranger in numerous Donald Duck and Humphrey Bear cartoons.

Even more animated was Jim Backus. A radio standard for over a decade on such series as *The Alan Young Show* (playing Hubert Updike), *The Danny Kaye Show, The Edgar Bergen And Charlie McCarthy Show, The Mel Blanc Show* and *Society Girl* (as Dexter Hayes), he began a brand new career in 1949 when he brought voice

to UPA's Mr. Magoo. In a few short years, Magoo had overshadowed all his previous work. It wasn't until he portrayed Thurston Howell III on *Gilligan's Island*, a variation of his Updike radio character, that he finally began to shake the Magoo image.

Many of the major voice artists for today's Cartoon Superstars honed their skills in countless radio series.

Teddy Bergman found fame on *The Fred Allen Show* playing an early resident on Allen's Alley known as Falstaff Openshaw, who recited such poems as "Back the patrol wagon to the sidewalk, Sergeant. That step's too high for my mother." The character was so amusing that he was spun off into his own radio series where Bergman and his son performed rhymed versions

Above:
Radio stars
Mortimer Snerd,
Charlie McCarthy
and Edgar
Bergen, and film
star Luana Patten
appear with the
animated stars of
Fun And Fancy
Free.
©Walt Disney
Company

of children's classics. Shortly thereafter, Bergman changed his name to Alan Reed and went on to become the original voice of Fred Flintstone.

During his radio days, Reed also performed frequently on *The Mel Blanc Show*, a radio series where talented voice artist Blanc ran a fix-it shop. Blanc supplied voice for many animated characters

PARDON THE INTERRUPTION, FOLKS, BUT I'M NOW BROADCASTING AN APPEAL FOR AN ONION, SOME SALT, A LITTLE PEPPER ETC

HAMBURGERS

I NOW PENETRATES TH' ETHER-WAVES, AN' I YAM USING ME STRENGTH FOR STRAGETY!

DINNER PAIL

FIRST YOU TAKE THE WHITES OF TWO EGGS— ETC. ETC ETC....

ZZOOM BAM POO ♪ POOOO♪

YE LUNCH WAGON

The Mel Blanc Show was a typical radio sitcom that gave Blanc the opportunity to showcase his vocal skill. At the beginning of the show, the announcer proclaimed, "... and starring the creator of the voice of Bugs Bunny..." followed by Mel saying, "Eh, what's up, Doc?" and the audience laughing and applauding.

In his biography, Blanc notes that when he was confined to his bed after a car accident, he was still able to record Barney Rubble's lines with the other actors standing around his bed partly because he and Reed had radio training together along with Bea Benadaret, the original voice of Betty Rubble, who also appeared regularly on Blanc's radio show. *The Flintstones* were able to continue without a hitch in this disastrous situation thanks to the performers' earlier experience of working together in radio. On radio, Blanc also did the voice of Sad Sack, the army private based on ex-Disney artist's George Baker's comic strip, as well as doing the voice of Woody Woodpecker.

Another Fred Allen regular, Kenny Delmar, after having his Senator Claghorn "borrowed" for Foghorn Leghorn, actually began doing voices in cartoons. His best known character would be "The Hunter" from the old *Underdog* series. Once again, his blustery, Southern

including Bugs Bunny, Daffy Duck, the original Woody Woodpecker, and much later

the voices for Barney Rubble (*The Flintstones*) and *Heathcliff*.

style voice made the most of this dog character who continually found himself chasing the crooked, and crafty fox.

June Foray, the voice of Rocky the Flying Squirrel and countless other characters worked on such series as, *The Buster Brown Gang*, and *The Fitch Bandwagon* (with Phil Harris, a top radio band leader and comic, best known as the voice of Baloo in Disney's *Jungle Book*) .

Arthur Q. Bryan also had a wide career on radio. He appeared as Wamond Wadcliffe on *The Fitch Bandwagon*, as Doc Gamble on *Fibber McGee And Molly Show* and as Major Hoople in *Major Hoople* based on the "Our Boarding House" comic strip by Gene Ahern (which also starred Mel Blanc as Mr. Twiggs). He also voiced regular roles on *The Great Gildersleeve* and others. In animation he is best known as the original voice of Elmer Fudd. It is interesting to wonder if the name "Fudd" came from the name "Fuddle" who was a neighbor on the *Blondie* radio show, portrayed by Bryan.

Of course no medium is a one way transfer. Just as cartoons borrowed from radio for voices, characters and dialogue, radio tried borrowing some characters from cartoons. As mentioned, radio borrowed from many sources for shows. There were shows

based on books, movies, pulp stories, comic strips and comic books. It was only natural that some shows would be borrowed from cartoons. However, this transfer was usually not successful .

Few radio series based solely on an animated character or series lasted any length. For this reason, copies of the shows are quite rare. Regrettably, little is known about some of these shows and as a result they are often merely a one sentence footnote in some of the discussions of these characters. There is even the chance that some animated stars's appearances on radio are totally forgotten.

Betty Boop had her chance with *Betty Boop Fables*. According to Fleischer historian Leslie Cabarga, this radio show only lasted for one year during the mid-Thirties. Mae Questel, the voice of the cartoon character from 1931-39, supplied Betty's voice for the radio show. Her companion, Ferdie Frog, was originally voiced by "Red Pepper Sam" Costello (the original voice for the animated Popeye) and who was replaced by Jack Mercer (a storyman at Fleischers who also inherited the voice role of the animated Popeye). Victor Erwin's orchestra provided the background music as it did for the *Popeye* radio show, and reportedly the Fleischer animated shorts as

Opposite Page: Promotional art for the Popeye radio show. © 1935 King Features

well.

Animation scholars have been searching unsuccessfully for years to find transcription disks of Betty Boop Fables. A major problem was that the disks made of radio shows in the 1920s and 1930s were done on a glass base which was very fragile and broke easily. By the 1940s, the base was being made of metal or acetate which is why most of the radio shows that still exist today came from the later years.

Walt Disney's famous rodent got his own radio show from NBC in 1937, *The Mickey Mouse Theater Of The Air*. Walt himself was credited as doing the voice of Mickey Mouse. Though Walt did provide the voice for the show there are some episodes where an educated ear can tell that some other voice artist was used for the world's most famous mouse. Clarence Nash did the voice of Donald Duck, just as he did in the animated cartoons. Goofy was performed by Stuart Buchman, Minnie Mouse was Thelma Boardman and Clarabelle Cow was Florence Gill. While Felix Mills' orchestra was credited with the music, there were also appearances by "Donald Duck's Swing Band" and "The Minnie Mouse Woodland Choir." Donald Duck's Swing Band sounded similar to the musical hijinks of Spike Jones (whose style was

copied in the Disney short, *Symphony Hour*).

The stories usually involved the familiar Disney characters taking a trip to someplace and visiting characters from popular nursery rhymes like the Old Woman in the Shoe or Old King Cole. One time Mickey and his friends even ventured under the sea to help King Neptune. Bill Demling was credited with the writing chores.

The Mickey Mouse Theater didn't last very long. However, numerous Disney characters appeared on radio

*Above:
The Superman radio show goes nationwide.
©1991 DC Comics, Inc.*

shows as "guests." One of the more extensive appearances had Walt Disney and Donald Duck guest on the *Edgar Bergen And Charlie McCarthy Show*. The episode was largely a plug for the then current *Fun And Fancy Free*. In the feature, one segment has Bergen telling the story of Jack and the Beanstalk to Charlie, Mortimer and Luana Patten, a child star who had also appeared in Disney's *The Song Of The South*. (Bergen's attempts to tell a story, only to be continually interrupted by Bergen, were

a standard feature on the show.) The radio show featured Donald and Walt talking with Edgar, Charlie and others on the series and then went into a version of "Mickey and the Beanstalk" in which Donald was assisted by Charlie and Ray Noble (the show's orchestra leader, and composer of some of the film's music).

Disney's *Snow White And The Seven Dwarfs* was dramatized on the *Lux Radio Theater* in December 1938. Many movies were dramatized on radio to increase public awareness of the film. This particular radio series was hosted by famed movie producer/director Cecil B. DeMille. Walt Disney, himself, appeared as a guest on the program and was interviewed by DeMille.

Though Popeye was a comic strip, his animated adventures added immeasurably to the sailor's popularity. The comic strip by E.C. Segar was credited as the basis of this radio show sponsored by Wheatena which premiered over NBC in 1935. Popeye's voice was supplied by Det Poppen and later Floyd Buckley. Olive Oyl was performed by Olive La Moy and later Mae Questel (the voice of the animated Olive). Jimmy Donnelly was "Matey, a newsboy adopted by Popeye" and Charles Lawrence did Wimpy. The music was by "Victor Erwin's Cartoonland Band." Additional voices included Everett Sloane, a popular actor with Orson Welles' Mercury Theater troupe and later the voice of Dick Tracy in UPA's cartoons of the Sixties.

Superman, the strange visitor from the planet Krypton debuted on the Mutual radio network in 1940. Kellogg's Pep cereal sponsored the program which followed the comic book adventures. Robert and Jessica Maxwell as well as George Lowther were listed as producers-writers-

directors. Lowther was responsible for the first Superman novel and also performed for a time as the narrator of the show. Superman/Clark Kent was voiced by Clayton "Bud" Collyer. Lois Lane was Joan Alexander and the best known narrator was Jackson Beck. Jackson Beck also voiced the radio role of "Beanie" the office boy for the series as well as doing the vocal chores for the animated Bluto and Brutus in the Fleischer/Famous/King Popeye cartoons. (For the record, Michael Fitzmaurice also performed Superman/Clark Kent.)

Collyer also performed as voice for the Man of Steel in the classic Fleischer cartoons. Collyer, Alexandar and Beck repeated their vocal roles decades later when in the mid-Sixties Filmation decided to do an animated series based on Superman.

For *The Woody Woodpecker Show*, Mel Blanc provided the voice for the troublesome bird in this Mutual Network show just as he had for the first animated cartoons. His Warner Brothers contract prevented him for doing further vocal chores for the character's animated escapades but it allowed him to play Woody on the air and also on a series of records. The show was reportedly broadcast in the late Forties.

By the mid-Fifties,

Next Page: Bea Benadaret and Mel Blanc, the original voices behind Betty and Barney Rubble, had worked together in radio. © Hanna-Barbera

television had supplanted radio's hold on a mass audience. Many radio series attempted to make the transition to television. A few succeeded, but most simply faded away not only from TV but from memory. Radio found itself converting to the format of recorded music hosted by disc jockeys. While there are some organizations today devoted to preserving the memories of those radio days, many of the original programs are lost forever. Despite the continuing popularity of Cartoon Superstars like Betty Boop, Woody Woodpecker and Mickey Mouse among others, it is difficult if not impossible to find records or cassettes from their radio shows.

Some of the golden age of radio is available from various sources on either tape or lp (and even Laserdisc!). Dealers that carry them include Filmfax Products, Box 1900, Evanston, IL 60204; Sandy Hook/Radiola, Box C, Sandy Hook, CT 06482; Jim Harmon, PO Box 38612, Hollywood, CA 90038; McCoy's Recording, PO Box 1069, Richland, WA 99352. Interested readers can write for their current catalogs.

Without radio, animation might have suffered. Radio supplied the inspiration for voices and characters, provided training ground for voice artists who would later be responsible for

75

memorable animated characters, and even gave audiences an opportunity to enjoy new adventures of their favorite characters. Though largely forgotten today, radio programming definitely made waves. Radio waves, that is! I say, that's a joke, son.

CHAPTER SEVEN:

CARTER'S LANDING: THE LOST STUDIO OF THE EIGHTIES

Forgotten animation studios abound in the history of cartoons. Van Beuren produced dozens of shorts in the Thirties that starred such characters as Tom and Jerry (two humans), Felix the Cat and Toonerville Trolley (a popular comic strip of the time). Ub Iwerks, who helped Disney create Mickey Mouse, opened his own studio and brought life to Flip the Frog and Willie Whopper.

When TV entered the picture, dozens of small studios sprang up to supply product. Some merely animated commercials. These studios' resumes would include Crusader Rabbit, Q.T. Hush, Courageous Cat, Tony the Tiger, the Ipana Beaver, and others. Though the studio names are forgotten, the product lives on. As more than one film historian has stated, the advantage of film over live performance is that once the performance is "in the can" it is there for all posterity. (This is not quite true, since there are many "lost" and forgotten films and TV series.)

From 1981 to 1983 there was an animation studio based in Newport Beach, California. It had art studios in Studio City, Burbank and Newport Beach. Its offices were often rich and luxurious. Its ever growing talent pool included top veterans and promising newcomers. Its work included animated features, theatrical shorts, TV specials, Saturday morning programming, amusement parks, interactive laser discs, children's books, comic strips and comic books.

It just never finished anything...

Tom Carter Productions did not have the most unusual studio history in animation, but it certainly had one of the saddest. It all began in 1981 when Tom Carter, a self-made millionaire, decided it would be a great idea to build a hotel-amusement park complex in Las Vegas. Carter had worked in the entertainment division of Disneyland during the late 1960s and early 1970s. After that he had gone into several business ventures, the most profitable being Medical "factoring."

Right: Licensing brochure cover showing Ol' Mudd's home. Painting by Michael Humphries. ©1983 Tom Carter Enterprises

"Factoring" is an investment plan based upon the purchase of unpaid bills. When there is an industry in which payment is slow, such as medical insurance payments, an entrepreneur will offer a doctor a percentage of the amount the doctor is owed to "take over" the bills. The doctor would receive immediate cash, often helpful. The purchaser then waits for the insurance company to pay in full, making a profit.

Carter took this money making practice and went a step further, selling shares to others. The idea being the additional income would allow him to buy up more bills. He would pay the investors a good rate, but take a little off the top for his time and effort. Investors were promised to make over 10% on their investment, a minimum of $5,000.

Having made millions in this field, Carter craved to use that cash to get back into entertainment. He began gathering a staff: Half of them to assist in his factoring business, the other half to help develop his entertainment ideas. One of the first of the creative group was Don Payne.

Payne had worked with Carter in Entertainment at Disneyland. He began working with Carter on both the factoring and the park. Joining Payne in quick procession were two other ex-Disneyland performers/

writers, Wally Boag and Jim Adams. Wally Boag was the famed vaudeville performer who helped creat the Golden Horseshoe Revue at Disneyland. For years he was listed in the *Guinness Book of World Records* for longest performance. Boag's legion of fans included top funnyman Steve Martin who studied Boag's vaudeville skills like making balloon animals. Adams had been Boag's understudy and replacement for years. The fourth member of the creative team, John Cawley, had also worked at Disneyland in the Entertainment division and as a Jungle Cruise operator. He had also worked at the Disney Studios in the Studio Archives.

Carter had been working with various individuals on designs for the attraction. He had purchased a parcel of land in Las Vegas near the current airport. Like Disney, Carter felt the park needed some form of background and theme. His idea was to build the entire concept around the Mark Twain character of Huckleberry Finn. The park was to be called "Huck's Landing" and would feature a water park atmosphere with old fashioned paddleboat as a restaurant and various water slides and rides.

One of the parties he was talking with about the park had an artist on staff, Phil Mendez. According to one

Above: Costumes of the key characters, like The Colonel, were produced. ©1983 Tom Carter Enterprises

source, the two went out for a drink together, and over drinks Mendez and Carter came up with the prospect of turning the park concept into an animated feature. The idea was that the feature would build awareness for the park and vice versa. It was an idea that had worked for Disney when he used the *Disneyland* TV show to promote Disneyland. Carter was sold and Mendez found

Carter's Landing: The Lost Studio Of The Eighties

himself a new partner.

Mendez began to set up a staff in Los Angeles to handle the production. His team put together a rough storyboard of the feature film. This original team included such veteran talent as Floyd Norman and Leo Sullivan. Norman had begun his career at Disney's in the Fifties and has since worked at numerous studios doing writing and development. Leo Sullivan had also worked at numerous studios.

*Below:
Cel set-up featuring Belvedere.
©1983 Tom Carter Enterprises*

The pair actually had their own educational film studio for a short period in the Sixties. The team presented the story to Carter in one of Mendez's crew's home as no studio location had yet been secured.

The story built a new legend around the Huck figure. The scenario followed Huck being lost on the Mississippi river when his mother accidentally drops him overboard. He is rescued by a turtle (Old

*Opposite page:
The cast of Tom Carter's Huck's Landing animated feature.
©1983 Tom Carter Enterprises*

Mudd) who cares for the boy. Mudd is continually warning Huck about a local raven who is more interested in having fun than learning to grow up.

The villain of the piece was an evil Quadroon (a white person with one-quarter Black blood). His attempts to capture the boy for the reward make for most of the tension. Also thrown in are an old man (Old Finn, where Huck gets his new last name), river pirates (whom the Quadroon sells Huck to), the Quadroon's river rats and Tom Sawyer.

Carter and his team were impressed with visual imagery seen in the art, but not in the story. All felt it was far too similar to a variety of Disney films including *Jungle Book* and *Rescuers*. However, it seemed a strong starting point and the project was officially off the ground.

The first studio was a small building on Ventura Boulevard in Studio City. The studio began work on two projects, *Huck's Landing* (the animated feature) and *Kissyfur*. *Kissyfur* was a creation of Mendez's about a father bear and his son. The original intent behind *Kissyfur* was to be a series of theatrical short subjects. These were to fill the artists' time when not working on the feature. It was Carter's and Mendez's belief that new animated shorts would

prove popular in theaters.

Mendez began to assemble his team which included several young artists who had little or no experience in the industry. Mendez told Carter that by training the animators themselves, they would save money. Carter wondered if using such untrained people might slow the production. According to Mendez, the artists would start slowly in animation, but would begin picking up speed, almost doubling their output each month. (This is a concept known as a "learning curve" which has been used on Disney features like *Roger Rabbit*. Unfortunately, in animation, the curve never raises as high as promised.) Carter was satisfied and spent a majority of his time in Newport Beach with his crew working on the Las Vegas project.

Time passed and a number of presentations were made to Carter on the feature. Few met with total success. At one time it was suggested the entire film be shot against 3-D backgrounds. This process was done in some early Fleischer cartoons (such as the two-reel *Popeye Meets Sinbad The Sailor*) and eventually was used in the British animated feature *When The Wind Blows* (1986). Each time the story was presented it was altered and characters appeared and disappeared. Beautiful

BELVEDERE ™

THE BARON ™

OL' MUDD ™

HUCK ™

BEULAH ™

PIERRE ™

TRACY ™

COLONEL ™

MISSY ™

ALFIE ™

background keys were being painted. Enormous story material was being drawn and tossed away.

When several of Carter's Newport Beach people began to question the progress on the feature, Mendez suggested that people who were not animators could not understand the animation process. He convinced Carter the best route would be to keep the Newport Staff away from the animation staff totally so they could work on the film. It was soon discovered that one reason for the slow progress on the feature was that workers at the Mendez studio were not working full time on the Carter projects.

Meanwhile, the Studio City studio had outgrown its small housing and moved to a large building in Burbank. Work was now expanding at the studio. Carter had a division working on TV specials and Saturday morning materials. Close to the Burbank Airport, this building flooded during the first major rain.

Along with all this expansion, the studio went through a number of cutbacks. Budget and creative differences made the work area somewhat unstable. Unfortunately, the work coming out was not what Carter wanted. Carter felt that whether his ideas were right or wrong, he was writing the checks and

wanted more of his input taken seriously.

An example of this "crossed purposes" was when the studio finished a *Kissyfur* short before they had finished any animation on *Huck's Landing.* On top of that, rather than having the short feature the cute "Winnie the Pooh" type bear, as seen in Mendez's original drawings (and later on the Saturday morning series *Kissyfur*) the short was a wild homage to Warners and MGM. Filled with violent gags and extreme takes, the short was amusing, but not what had been discussed. This film never went beyond the rough cut phase.

Eventually, Mendez left the operation. He gave up his claim to the *Huck's*

Right: Original cel drawing of Kissyfur disguised as queen bee for Carter's unreleased theatrical short. ©1983 Tom Carter Enterprises

Landing concept and Carter relinquished any claim to *Kissyfur.* (Mendez later sold the concept to NBC as a Saturday morning series.) Mendez was briefly replaced by Leo Sullivan. Carter's Newport Staff convinced Carter that they should take some control over the production. They argued that the film was really only one part of the Carter/Huck's Landing plan. Also on their side was that John Cawley did have knowledge of animation production. Carter gave his creative team a chance and they wrote a new script for the film. Carter approved of the storyline and the Newport Team took control of the project.

The new story took the focus away from a "boy

raised by animals" theme to one of returning home. The main set pieces for the new film included a gigantic riverboat disaster of which the only known survivor is Huck. There were to be several quick vignettes of him growing in the wild, some with no dialogue. The heart of the film occurred when he finally sees another riverboat. This causes him to dream of living among his own people. He makes a raft and heads to the nearest town.

There, unfamiliar with the way of humans, he makes a number of mistakes that eventually lead to a saloon brawl. A fire breaks out and Huck not only remembers his origin, but recognizes the man who created the ship disaster. Huck is recognized by the villain (now changed to a once distinguished "Baron"). A chase ensues through the river country. The island animals come to rescue Huck, though it is Huck who finally conquers the villain.

After a brief farewell to his island friends, Huck goes back to the humans to introduce himself.

This newer story (which in some ways has many of the elements that later proved so successful in 1989's *The Little Mermaid*) was somewhat overlong. That was due to an incredible amount of past baggage. When the new writers first started, they focused on a newer, smaller set of secondary characters than Mendez had envisioned. Unfortunately, there were certain elements and characters that Carter insisted be put back into the tale. Though long, the script did contain solid, well defined characters and good flow of action.

Gerry Ray was brought in to head up the feature. Ray had had a long career in animation going back to the 1950s. He had directed many of the Jay Ward cartoons from the Mexican studio set up with Ward. Ray returned to the US in the late 1970s

Above: Sample proposed daily comic strip based on the characters in Huck's Landing. ©1983 Tom Carter Enterprises

where he worked on a variety of shows, commercials and features. Ray read the new script and thought it had strong potential.

With a new head in charge of the feature, Carter decided to move the entire operation to Newport Beach. He assisted those who wanted to make the move. Some artists preferred to continue living in the Los Angeles area and were granted special hours so they needn't make the commute every day.

In Newport Beach, the projects were divided up amongst the staff so that better control could be maintained. Ray oversaw the feature. Other talent involved included animation workhorse Chuck Harvey and key background talent Mike Humphries. Stephanie Burke, a painting supervisor was promoted to production manager.

The music was being written by Don Dorsey and Adam Bezark. Dorsey had

Carter's Landing: The Lost Studio Of The Eighties

Other proposals included an obnoxious whale and his inept hunter.

A problem with the Newport based studio was Carter's work manner. He would stop production at any moment to have the entire team work on something else he deemed more important. There was also a great deal of time given to Carter's various outside interests. (One artist was sent out to paint a mural for Carter's church.) All of this tended to give a disjointed feeling to the staff.

Almost frame, by frame, work continued. The script was slowly storyboarded even with continual plot twists thrown in by Carter who had "new ideas" frequently. Licensing deals with a variety of major toy and product companies were signed. Character costumes of some of the animated characters were constructed. Songs were written for the film. Animation cycles were prepared. Comic book versions of the film and Saturday morning shows began production. Even a comic strip based on the characters of *Huck's Landing* was developed.

Amidst this continual progress, the studio moved again. This time the entire Carter organization moved to a building of their own in Irvine. Originally an architectural firm's building, this new setting was the most luxurious of probably

worked for Quincy Jones and Disneyland (where he was one of the key people behind the music for the popular Electrical Parade). Quincy Jones heard much of the music and thought it would be one of the richest animated scores every produced.

Scott Shaw!, well known for his comic book and animation work, was in charge of the Saturday

Above: Scott Shaw!'s cover to Carter's proposed comic book featuring Alex in Wonderland. ©1987 Scott Shaw!

morning crew and later a comic books division. He worked with comic legend Mike Sekowsky (who had worked on such titles as *The Justice League of America, Wonder Woman,* and *Bwana Beast*), Floyd Norman and Dawn Miller. The projects included a crazy series based on a boy who falls into his TV set, *Alex In Wonderland.* It was a sort of *Alice In Wonderland* meets *TRON.*

any animation studio in history: glass ceilings in the lobby, an elegant winding staircase at the entrance, fine wood and furnishings everywhere. There was a full kitchen, a swimming pool and even a sauna! The animation staff made continual jokes about the elaborate surroundings and the almost too numerous potted plants which gave the rooms almost a jungle atmosphere.

Then, in November of 1983 this world of fantasy ended. It occurred over the Thanksgiving holiday when a local newspaper broke a story about Carter allegedly being investigated regarding the legality of his "factoring" operation. Reports allegedly labeled the business akin to a pyramid scheme. (This is where early investors are paid dividends that actually come from the funds of new investors.) There was talk of a Federal investigation into the "investment fraud" as one paper called it.

Employees were telephoned over the weekend and told to take an extra holiday on the following Monday. Before that Monday was over, they were told to come immediately to the building. It was to be locked shut by the courts. That night the artists, the park designers and others came to the building to pick up their personal belongings.

Sadly, it was reported that some used the time to take whatever they could grab with some employees reportedly walking out with computers, recording equipment, furniture and more. Artists were allowed to take limited samples of their artwork for portfolio use. To quote one artist, "it was like those end of the world movies where everyone is yelling, and angry, and looting stores."

The Carter story is one of almost total loss. Many of those who were employed there at the time of the closing didn't get a final check. Those artists who had moved down there were now faced with having to re-locate back up to the Los Angeles area where the animation industry was. Then there are the hundreds of non-employees (and some employees) who lost their entire savings.

What happened to the trail of the studio afterwards is a winding, often broken string of bankruptcy councils, legal activity and occasional news. Years later, Carter, still untried, was attempting to get funds for some new land in Las Vegas and to produce an animated special on Huck's Landing. However, by 1990 the courts caught up and he began serving a jail sentence.

Besides the financial loss, many of the artists at the studio felt the loss of time. They had spent a great deal of time producing high quality material of which no one would ever see. It was almost as if they had been out of the business for several years. Those who showed the materials in their portfolio always received high praise for it.

Several studios expressed interest in a number of Carter's TV ideas. The feature script was shown around for various reasons. Frank Thomas and Ollie Johnson, two of Disney's "Nine Old Men," remarked that the script was one of the strongest stories they'd seen in animation since working with Walt Disney. Don Bluth felt the script showed high animation potential and allegedly expressed interest in working on it. Sadly, all of that material was (and probably still is) controlled by whatever entities ended up with the Carter legal property. All the studio property of animation desks (specially made for Carter), art materials and such were auctioned off shortly after the shutdown.

Gerry Ray, whose credits in the business are well known, (and abbreviated in this article) died during the final days of Carter. Ray had been diagnosed with cancer shortly after meeting with the Carter people. When he discovered his illness he told Carter and his Newport Crew that he would withdraw his offer to head the feature since he might have some medical problems near the end. Carter's team unanimously agreed that Ray could helm the feature as long as he (Ray) felt he could. His final days were in a hospital where fellow employees never really let him know what was happening at the studio. Ray felt that as soon as he got out of the hospital he would get right to work on the feature. Ray never left the hospital.

The entire Carter experience is viewed nowadays as almost an industry joke. There are snide allusions to the Carter Studio (or the "Newport Beach Studio") made when one discusses shaky production companies. The most common thoughts are

Below right: Rough sketch of Ol' Mudd. ©1982 Tom Carter Enterprises

Below: Brochure for investors in the Huck's Landing concept, not for Carter's factoring business. ©1983 Tom Carter Enterprises

always questions about "whatever happened to" the non-animation studio staff. Those who worked there still express a bitterness about the situation.

However, the Carter studio did offer many newcomers a chance to move up in the animation field. Tom Shannon, a local Orange County cartoonist, began doing illustrations at Carter and now works on Disney features. Stephanie Burke was an ink and paint supervisor who moved into production management at Carter and later held similar positions at Marvel Productions before becoming a key executive at the Fox Children's Network. There were a number of students who moved up the ranks and became key talents in the new boom of animation. The old pros, like the Floyd Normans, Scott Shaw!s and Gerry Rays were surrounded by such equally pro talent as the aforementioned Mike Sekowsky (famed comic book artist), Michael Humphries (key background painter for Disney and Hanna-Barbera) and Chuck Harvey (animator for Disney and almost every other studio.)

The studio really never produced anything the public saw. Carter's own desire to move in multiple directions kept him from completing anything before the forced shutdown. In many ways, he was a man of

vision. When Carter first proposed a family attraction in Las Vegas in 1981, he was truly ahead of his time. Currently there are no less than three such attractions being built or proposed, including a Universal Studio's tour. His belief that animated shorts would come back to theaters came true with Disney, 20th Century Fox and Warner Brothers all renewing the production of shorts in the late Eighties.

However the talent and time involved with Carter will keep his dreams from ever being totally forgotten, even if only as "the craziest place" a group of creators ever worked. Like some lost civilization, or the Loch Ness Monster, the Carter Studio will no doubt become a major mystery to animation researchers in future years who stumble across the name, but can find nothing to support the fact that it existed.

WHERE'S
THE
SPAT OF
MARGE?

TOP SE-CRET

CHAPTER EIGHT:

PRIME TIME
ANIMATION B.S.
(BEFORE SIMPSONS)

Prime Time Animation B.S. (Before Simpsons)

Despite all the media publicity, *The Simpsons* may not be as unique as all those articles in newspapers and magazines claim. A prime time animated series is nothing new. Even a ground breaking, popular, prime time animated series is nothing new.

Ever since *The Flintstones* debuted three decades ago in 1960, animation has been attempting to fight its way into the world of prime time. All those articles on *The Simpsons* seem to only recall *The Flintstones* and ignore the many other attempts to catch the attention of both an adult and child audience with animation. Many popular animated series got their start in prime time, not on

Below:
Disney's ABC series was the main source for prime time animation in the Fifties.
© 1991 Walt Disney Company

Saturday morning. Heroes like *Top Cat, Jonny Quest and Alvin and the Chipmunks* began their careers entertaining night time audiences.

In an interview, *Simpson's* creator Matt Groening stated, "As a kid, I'd watch *Ed Sullivan* and *Walt Disney* on Sunday night and discuss it the next day in school. Kids are now doing that with *The Simpsons.*" As in many areas of animation, Disney was first.

The first series to feature animation in the late night arena was *The Disney TV Show.* It began in 1954 and changed titles a number of times from *Disneyland* to *Walt Disney Presents* to *Walt Disney's Wonderful World Of Color* to the present day *The Wonderful World Of Disney.* This show often featured animation. It originated the format of having several classic cartoons tied together with new surrounding animation. The show sparked the creation of a new Disney animated character, *Ludwig Von Drake,* and demonstrated a night time audience was willing to watch animation.

Previously, animation was a daytime affair with reruns of theatrical cartoons that appeared on local stations. Hanna-Barbera offered all new animation with *The Huckleberry Hound Show.* The show was a hit and often ran quite late in the day. However, other than

the few commercials, prime time TV was virgin territory for animation.

The Fall of 1960 changed all that when ABC, at that time the lowest rated network, debuted three new animated series: *The Bugs Bunny Show, Matty's Funday Funnies* and *The Flintstones.* These three series were perfect examples of basic animation programming.

Matty's Funday Funnies (ABC/Friday/7:30) actually debuted the previous year, but in a 5:00 time slot. The program was composed of some of the old Famous/ Paramount/Harvey cartoons with characters like Casper, Herman & Katnip, Little Audrey and the Noveltoons crew like Buzzy the Crow. The show had animated hosts, Matty Mattel And Sister Sue Belle, who helped hawk all those fine toys from Mattel. In 1962, those old cartoons were replaced with new animation starring *Beany & Cecil.* Bob Clampett provided these new cartoons based on his popular puppet show *Beany & Cecil. Matty* was canceled in December 1962, but *Beany & Cecil* enjoyed a healthy career in reruns as a weekend morning show.

The Bugs Bunny Show (ABC/Tuesday/7:30) was similar to the Disney series with classic cartoons being given a unifying theme thanks to some new wraparound animation. The series lasted for two seasons.

These shows were directed by Chuck Jones and Friz Freleng and captured some of the style of the classic Warners work. After a classy opening song (*Overture! Curtain! Lights! This Is It The Night Of Nights...*), Bugs took the stage to introduce the cartoons. Many of the wraparound stories dealt with Daffy Duck wanting to take over the hosting chores from Bugs Bunny or the guest host. In one episode, Daffy disguises himself as Bugs, gets stuck in the rabbit suit and is chased by a sheep dog who thinks Daffy is a rabbit. This story line continued in between showing three classic Warner cartoons. Guest hosts would include characters like Pepe LePew, the skunk, who discussed Paris and love and Tweety who had to have his cage nailed to the ceiling to be safe from Sylvester. Unfortunately, these wonderful compilations haven't been seen in over a decade.

The Flintstones (ABC/ Friday/8:30) was a real milestone as it garnered as strong an adult audience as the usual children viewers. It was not unusual to have commercials with Fred and Barney selling Winston cigarettes because this was supposedly an *adult* show. Unlike the other two series, it was not based upon established cartoon characters, but original creations. Hanna-Barbera's

MATTY'S FUNNIES with BEANY and CECIL

modern stone age family took the nation by storm with a merchandising boom and laudatory articles in newspapers and magazines.

The April 1961 issue of *TV Radio Mirror* magazine declared, "The impossible happened this television season, when a cartoon series jumped into second place in national ratings. Into a TV world dominated by cowboys, private eyes and neurotic villains came *The Flintstones*, an 'animated' family show as wholesome as a fresh apple."

Even in the midst of the television animation boom of the early Sixties, it was as difficult to bring *The Flintstones* to life as it was in

*Above:
Bob Clampett's
sea-sick serpent
replaced old
Harvey cartoons.
© Bob Clampett*

the late Eighties during a similar animation boom. In an early Sixties interview, Joe Barbera, writer-producer of the show, commented, "*The Flintstones* were hard to develop. In the first place, no one had ever heard of a cartoon series in the evenings, when adults are home. We thought it could be done because Yogi (Bear) and Huck (Hound) already had a tremendous adult following...(the networks) bought it immediately, and a top executive commented, 'At least this doesn't have blood running down the alley.'"

For its first season, it was rated 18, above such "hot" shows as *Alfred Hitchcock*

Prime Time Animation B.S. (Before Simpsons)

Presents, The Red Skeleton Show and even *Walt Disney Presents!* Critics lavished praise on this innovative show that was "inspired" by the live action sitcom *The Honeymooners.* Even in its second season, the show was still in the top 25, once again beating Walt Disney. The series would eventually run six years in prime time and for decades more in syndication. With its many spinoffs and specials, *The Flintstones* could arguably be considered the most successful TV series of all time either animated or live action.

Certainly there are many obvious comparisons between this show and *The Simpsons.* One of those areas of similarity is that other networks saw the success and attempted to duplicate it. The success of *The Simpsons* has caused other networks, including Fox itself, to think about other possible animated series that might work in prime time. Three decades ago, life wasn't much different.

The year 1961 saw another four shows introduced: *The Bullwinkle Show, The Alvin Show, The Calvin And The Colonel And Top Cat.* These shows were in addition to the three animated series already appearing in prime time, for an amazing total of seven prime time animated series. Like *The Flintstones,* the new shows this year featured

Right:
Rocky and Bullwinkle's move to prime time in The Bullwinkle Show garnered a cover in 1961.
© 1961 Jay Ward

mostly brand new characters, many of whom would become future stars. However, unlike *The Flintstones,* none of them would last beyond one season in prime time, although they would find further life in reruns on weekend mornings.

The Bullwinkle Show (NBC/sunday/7:00) was a revised and somewhat improved version of the *Rocky And His Friends* show seen since 1959 during the day. Rocky, the flying squirrel, was teamed with Bullwinkle Moose in serial adventures (two episodes per show). There were other segments on the show, some of them repeats from the earlier *Rocky And His Friends* including *Fractured Fairy Tales, Peabody's Improbably History,* and *Bullwinkle's Corner* alternating with *Mr. Know It All. The Bullwinkle Show* did have some new elements not on the original series. First, there was a new segment devoted to a staunch and true Royal Canadian Mounted policeman, Dudley Do-Right. Also, for the first few installments, there was a live action Bullwinkle puppet that gave cockeyed advice to children and was quickly eliminated from the show after the first few initial broadcasts, never to be seen again.

The Calvin And The Colonel (ABC/Tuesday/8:30) featured the talents of Freeman Gosden and Charles Correll, the team that had created one of the most popular radio shows ever broadcast-*Amos 'N' Andy*. Gosden and Correll were white performers but did Black dialect characters on the radio. When the show was transferred to TV, actual Black actors were used. Even by 1961, there were protests that *Amos 'N' Andy* promoted Black stereotyping. To see if they could continue their form of humor and yet avoid further protests, Gosden and Correll transformed their classic comic characters in Colonel Montgomery Klaxon, a clever fox, and Calvin Burnside, a cigar smoking bear, who was a little short of brains. Gosden and Correll provided the voices and had input into the stories. Today the show is barely remembered, if at all, by animation fans.

The Alvin Show (CBS/Wednesday/7:30) brought Alvin and the Chipmunks to the small screen. Though the Chipmunks are well known today, they were probably never better loved than in the late Fifties and early

Sixties. The success of their record, especially *The Chipmunk Song*, made them stars and almost as an afterthought, an animated series was developed about them. Alvin, a furry Dennis the Menace, along with his brothers, Simon and Theodore, gave their surrogate parent, David Seville a rough time. Pre-dating music videos, their adventures often involved them singing a song. An additional segment in the show was the misadventures of inventor Clyde Crashcup and his assistant Leonardo who both succeeded each week in inventing things that already existed.

Top Cat (ABC/Wednesday/8:30) was Hanna-Barbera's second prime time entry. Like *The Flintstones*, this series was "suggested" by another live action series: Phil Silver's *You'll Never Get Rich* (AKA *The SGT. Bilko Show*).Instead of cartooned humans, this time Hanna-Barbera went back to the standard funny animals they had handled so well. The series featured a group of alley cats led by Top Cat who were often in trouble with the local police because of their lifestyle and con jobs.

The failure of these series to mimic the success of *The Flintstones* no doubt caused networks to re-think the situation and decide *The*

Flintstones was probably just a lucky fluke that couldn't be reproduced. One last attempt was made in 1962 with the introduction of *The Jetsons* (ABC/Sunday/7:30). This Hanna-Barbera series blatantly tried to capture some of the elements that made *The Flintstones* a hit. There was a family setting, wild gadgets and a live action sitcom format. While *The Flintstones* still was going strong in prime time, this clever imitation only lasted one season although it did go on to receive greater recognition including a new syndicated series and a

Below: Prime Time series stars Calvin and the Colonel in their own comic book. © 1962 Kayro, Inc.

Above:
The animated
cast from Off
To See The
Wizard.
© MGM

Opposite page:
Hanna-Barbera's
Where's Huddles
was advertised as
a "sports situation
comedy."
© 1970
Hanna-Barbera

feature film.

It wasn't until 1964 that two networks again tried to use animation in prime time. *Jonny Quest* (ABC/Friday/7:30) was an innovative animated series. It tried, within a limited budget, to recapture the action adventure of the Tom Swift books or the early movie serials and their pulpish boy's adventure stories. Considering the limitations, the show, featuring serious animated humans in semi-realistic exploits, was an amazing achievement. It is one of Hanna-Barbera's best loved series.

Also in 1964 *The Famous Adventures Of Mr. Magoo* (NBC/Saturday/8:00) debuted. Inspired by the ratings success of *Mr. Magoo's Christmas Carol*,an hour long Christmas special where Mr. Magoo performed as Scrooge in the famous Charles Dickens' story, the network wrongly assumed that audiences would love to see Magoo perform in other famous stories. Much like a Classics Illustrated comic book transferred to TV, classic tales were trimmed for TV and Magoo suddenly found himself in the roles of Puck in *Midsummer's Night Dream,* Friar Tuck in "Robin Hood" and a host of other inappropriate parts. The character of Magoo was totally forgotten and the sources of Magoo's humor, his blindness and grouchiness, were completely ignored. The network had misjudged why the original Christmas special was so successful and as a result produced one of the oddest of all series for an animated star.

The Flintstones finally left prime time in 1966. Prime time was now filled with live action fantasy like *The Munsters, Get Smart, Lost In Space* among other shows. They offered to audiences that same fast-paced glimpse into unusual worlds that had been the special function of animation for many years.

Combinations of live action and animation were tried, all lasting a single season. *Off To See The Wizard* in 1967 featured live action children's films hosted by animated versions of the memorable characters from Oz. Hanna-Barbera experimented with live actors integrated with animated characters and animated backgrounds in *The New Adventures Of Huckleberry Finn* (1968). *My World And Welcome To It* (1969), based on the writings and drawings of James Thurber, frequently featured animated vignettes in the Thurber art style.

In the Seventies, Hanna-Barbera tried to invade prime time again. *Where's Huddles* premiered July of 1970 on CBS, Wednesday nights at 7:30. It was a mid season replacement and lasted less than a dozen episodes. The stories revolved around a football quarterback and his wife, Ed and Marge Huddles. Their friends were football center Bubba McCoy and his wife, Penny. Causing problems was a football hating next door neighbor,

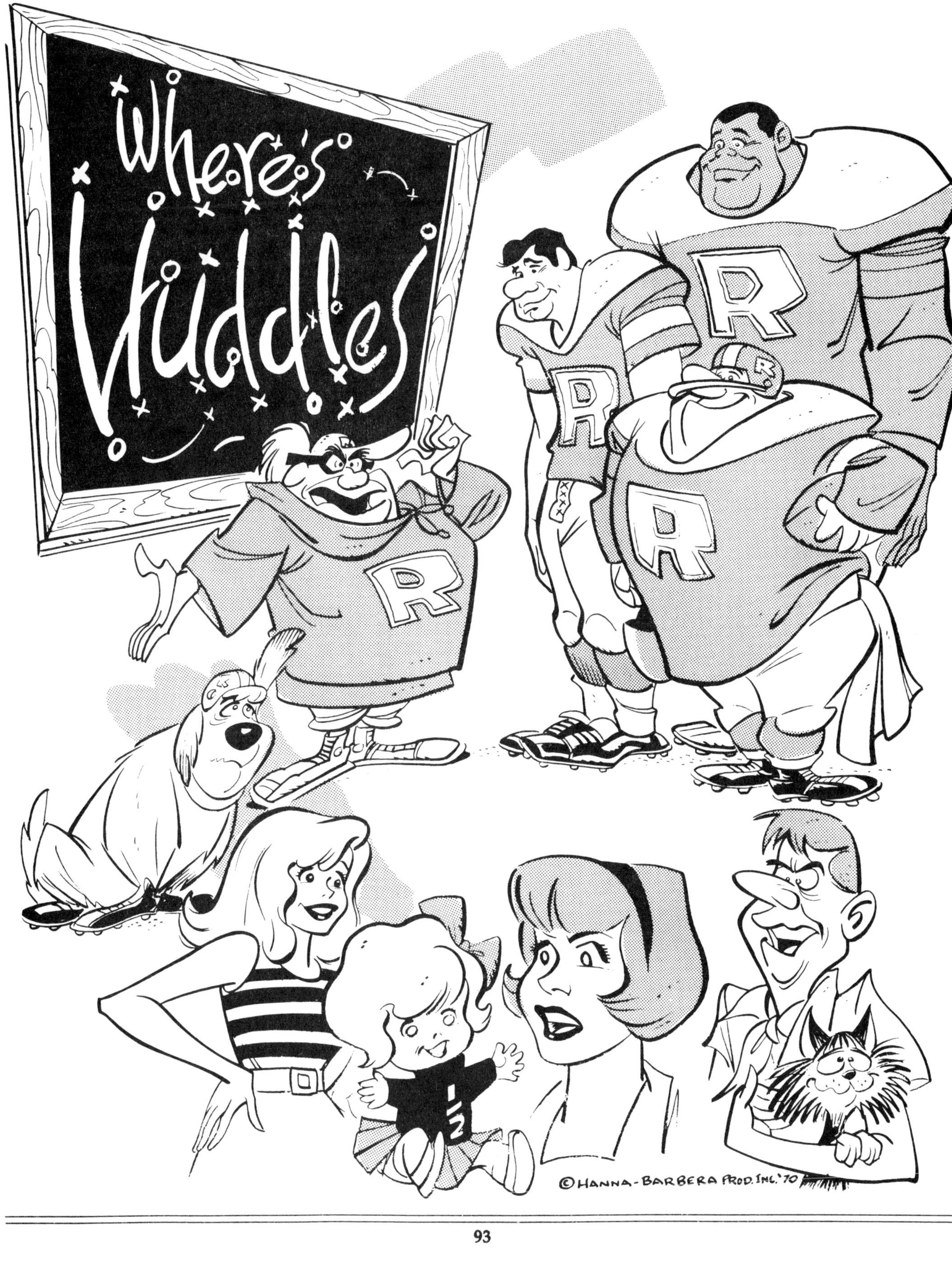
Where's Huddles
©HANNA-BARBERA PROD. INC. '70

Prime Time Animation B.S. (Before Simpsons)

Claude Pertwee, voiced by Paul Lynde.

In 1971, a major change took place on network TV. The networks were required to "give back" one half hour of programming to the local stations. Prime time suddenly began at 8:00 most nights. Special programming like news or family fare were allowed to begin earlier on weekends. Some tried to cash into this new time slot with animated projects. Hanna-Barbera offered *Wait*

Below: A dancing duck provides entertainment for a group of skeptical spectators in a "segment of animated jokes for mature audiences" from Hanna-Barbera's Jokebook. ©1982 Hanna-Barbera

Till Your Father Gets Home which ran two seasons (1972-74), while Disney brought in *The Mouse Factory* (1972).

Wait Till Your Father Gets Home had *Happy Day's* father Tom Bosley supplying the voice for Harry Boyle, owner of the Boyle Restaurant Supply Company, who got into conflicts with his family, especially his teenaged daughter who was an outspoken activist for many social causes. Some episodes in the second season had

guest appearances by caricatures of stars like Don Knotts, Jonathan Winters and Phyllis Diller with the voices provided by the actual performers.

Directed by Disney legend Ward Kimball, *The Mouse Factory* had a different live action host each week like Annette Funicello, Dom DeLuise, Don Knotts and Jim Backus involved in some framing story or central theme that allowed plenty of clips from Disney's animated cartoons and live action films. For example, one week Charles Nelson Reilly discussed vacations, illustrating his suggestions with scenes from Goofy cartoons.

Animation didn't return to prime time until Spring 1982. This time Hanna-Barbera tried a new type of animated show entitled *Jokebook.* It was scheduled on Fridays at 8:00 on NBC. The show was a series of animated vignettes. These "jokes" were meant to be "hip" and "adult," similar to the cartoons seen in magazines and newspapers. In an attempt to achieve a younger feel, Hanna-Barbera purchased student animated films for presentation on the show. In some respects, this series was as much a ground breaking animated series as was *The Flintstones* over two decades earlier. Though Hanna-Barbera produced five episodes of the series, only four aired due to the

dismal ratings. (This "lost" series is so totally forgotten that it doesn't appear on Hanna-Barbera's official studio list of shows. It didn't even get mentioned in the recent mega-buck book *The Art of Hanna-Barbera*.)

Animation in prime time was once again relegated to holiday specials and TV commercials. There were a few exceptions. One of Steven Spielberg's best received episodes of his critical and rating failed *Amazing Stories* (1985-87) was the animated *Family Dog* (1987) segment. This segment, directed and written by Brad Bird, was a series of three small vignettes about a small dog continually at a loss with its human family. This episode was so memorable that years later CBS commissioned a prime time series based on the episode to debut in 1991.

Spring 1989 saw the airing of Ralph Bakshi's *Hound Town* pilot on NBC. The series, which featured a dog's eye view of the world, was geared a bit more towards adults. The series didn't sell. Neither did 1990 attempts like *The Jackie Bison Show* (borrowed somewhat from the live action *Jack Benny Show*), about a buffalo talk show host and his typical situation comedy storyline about falling in love with the wrong woman. Also released in 1990 was *Hollywood Dog*, loosely based on an independent comic

strip, that combined live action with animation in a fashion similar to *Who Framed Roger Rabbit*. The animated Hollywood Dog helped a struggling live action singer-songwriter.

After almost 30 years, no series had been able to catch the public's eye as *The Flintstones* had...and then came *The Simpsons*. Unlike their prehistoric predecessors, *The Simpsons* did not merely burst onto the TV screen. They worked their way up to a series.

The Tracey Ullman Show, a variety program, was one of the Fox Networks first series. While in development, the producer of the show, James Brooks, approached *Life In Hell* cartoonist Matt Groening about the possibility of doing some animated segments. Some state that Brooks asked Groening if he had something without rabbits; a more popular tale is that Groening was reluctant to surrender control of the strip's characters to Fox. Either way, Groening created a new group of characters, *The Simpsons*, based on writings he had done in high school and named them after members of his own family. (Except for "Bart" which is an anagram for "brat.")

For the first three seasons of *The Tracey Ullman Show*, the Simpsons were used as segues in and out of commercial breaks. Originally these were four 15

to 20 second bits each with their own punchline but by the third season, it had evolved into a single segment of a self contained story lasting about a minute and a half. The Simpson family became stars but Fox was hesitant to spin them off into their own series. The network suggested perhaps four half hour specials during the year. However, Groening held out for a series and the network finally agreed to an order of 13 episodes (12 plus a Christmas special).

The Simpsons first appeared on December 17th, 1989, as a half hour Christmas special where Homer Simpson, the father, tries to earn extra money working as a Santa Claus. He blows all the money at the dog track in an ill fated attempt to increase his earnings, but still manages to give his family a merry Christmas. This special definitely established that the show's story and characters would be unlike *Father Knows Best* (although both families live in Springfield), even though the special harbored many of the same "family values" found in other holiday specials. The airing of the special gave the Fox Network one its highest ratings ever!

The actual series debuted on the Fox Network, Sunday, January 14, 1990 at 8:30 p.m. In the opener, Bart Simpson cheats on an intelligence test

HER SUPREME MOMNESS

and is sent to a school for gifted children. The show was the #1 rated show in a number of major cities including Los Angeles and New York. Nationally, the episode ranked third place amongst the four networks. Week two found the series in second place!

Magazines and newspapers were right when they claimed that not since *The Flintstones* had there been such nationwide excitement for a prime time animated TV series. Within months of its premiere in January 1990, the show racked up impressive ratings and cracked the list of the top 20 rated shows several times. They even won their time slot on a few occasions,

Above:
The Simpsons promote Mother's Day.
™ and © 1989 Twentieth Century Fox Film Corporation

beating out ABC, CBS, and NBC shows on at the same time. The show also had impressive demographics, with a strong adult audience tuning into the show as well as the teenagers and young children.

For its second season, Fox moved the show opposite NBC's *The Cosby Show,* the number one series for nearly a decade. Though the show continued with strong ratings, it was generally rated second in its time slot. (However, one night *The Simpsons* did beat Cosby and headlines heralded the news!) Talk began of a possible animated feature based on the series. (This would give it another "common" element with *The Flintstones* who starred in 1966's big screen *The Man Called Flintstone.*)

Hopefully *The Simpsons* will continue on with their own growth in popularity and in ratings. The more publicity it receives the more it will help animation in general. As mentioned earlier, several networks are already considering animated series for prime time slots. Fox is thinking of airing another series, CBS is looking at a new Pink Panther-live action combination series and other networks have various projects in development. Series ranging from *Capital Critters,* about the vermin (mice, rats, and roaches) in the basement of the White

House, to *Fish Police,* based on a popular independent comic book series (*Fish Police*), are being developed.

It's surprising some independent stations haven't started using some of their highly rated animated series (such as *Teenage Mutant Ninja Turtles, Tale Spin,* or *Tiny Toon Adventures*) to "counter program" in an early prime time period against the networks ragged schedule of sappy sitcoms and absurd action shows. (At least one independent began "counter programming" against *The Simpsons;* it aired the original *Bullwinkle Show* opposite it!)

In April of 1991, CBS scheduled an early prime time slot for a rotating series of animated special presentations featuring such popular characters as Bugs Bunny, Teenage Mutant Turtles, the Peanuts gang and others.

It will be interesting to see if *The Simpsons* will have the staying power of *The Flintstones.* In particular whether these new kids on the block can break the six season prime time record held by *The Flintstones.* As Homer Simpson might say, "No problemo!"

TOP SECRET

CHAPTER NINE:

HOW TO MAKE A HIT ANIMATED FEATURE

How To Make A Hit Animated Feature

Being in a list of the top ten, twenty, or even 500 (as in *Fortune 500*) is often viewed as a sign of true success; especially when the list refers to money being made. Those who make the lists become the role models for those still struggling. As is often the case, what's true in the real world is true in the world of entertainment and animation.

Ever since Steven Spielberg's *Jaws* (1975) grossed over $100 million in its first release, movie makers and the public have taken more and more of an interest in how much movies make. Since that time, many films have crossed the $100 million mark. A smaller number of films that have topped $200 million with *E.T.* being the highest grossing film in history with over $300 million.

As important as the final figure is the first weekend's performance. A film's economic future is often based on whether it made as much money "as expected" on its opening weekend. A film doing well at the box-office spurs more interest in seeing the film, and thus the film does even better. The film that makes "less than expected" on its opening weekend is viewed as a problem film and will generally do less and less each week.

The $100 million mark has yet to be reached by an animated feature, but Steven

Spielberg's *E.T.* and Disney's *The Little Mermaid* do have something financially in common. They are both number one on lists of top grossing films of all time. Not to say that the lists are the same. The list for "top ten grossing features" is quite different than that for "top ten grossing animated features." Animated features don't even appear in the top thirty of the general "top grossing" list. The highest is usually Disney's *Snow White*, the amount being accumulated from all releases from the film.

Those who make and sell animation pay more attention to the list of top grossing animated features. It's this list that helps studios determine what topics "sell" in animation. Studios use this list to help choose future story ideas. They also point to it when trying to interest prospective backers.

For this reason, those features that make the top ten list affect all future features. The creative people

*Below:
Trade ad noting film history.
© 1991 Walt Disney Company*

involved with them will be in big demand, even if their actual participation was small. Producers who come up with stories that seem to fit into the list think they will have an easier time selling the film. More than one producer has stated that his "current" project was chosen because it was so similar to "other" top ten films. In fact two on the top ten list have sequels in production.

So what are the films that will have the greatest effect on the future of animated features?

Before we begin with that examination, we'll state that all the grosses (money made) for the following films were made only during the year listed. This dispenses with the misleading Disney box-office records in which Disney adds one release to another until suddenly a film like *Snow White* is listed with a gross of over $150 million dollars (having earned it in nearly a dozen reissues).

Also, only films released during the Eighties (1981-1990) are considered. This eliminates the old argument that you can't compare films of the Forties with those of the Eighties due to the fact that ticket prices were far cheaper in decades past. This also gives a bit more insight into the modern film audience's tastes.

Finally, here is the list of the 20 top money making animated features of the

Eighties. After the title is the studio that produced it and the year of release. (An "r" following the release year indicates that it is actually a re-issue.) The final figure is the estimated final box-office gross. (The producing studio will usually see only one-third of that amount.)

Top Grossing Animated Features Of the 1980s:

1. *The Little Mermaid* (Disney/1989) 84.3
2. *Oliver & Company* (Disney/1988) 48.1
3. *Snow White* (Disney1987 R/50th Anniversary) 46.6
4. *The Land Before Time* (Spielberg-Lucas-Bluth/ 1987) 46.0
5. *An American Tail* (Spielberg-Bluth/1986) 45.8
6. *The Jungle Book* (Disney/1990R) 44.5
7. *Bambi* (Disney/1988R) 39.0
8. *Cinderella* (Disney/1987R) 34.1
9. *101 Dalmatians* (Disney/1985R) 31.2
10. *Lady And The Tramp* (Disney/1986R) 31.1
11. *Peter Pan* (Disney/1989R) 29.4
12. *All Dogs Go To Heaven* (Sullivan Bluth/1989) 26.2
13. *Pinocchio* (Disney/1984R) 26.0
14. *The Great Mouse Detective* (Disney/1986) 25.1
15. *Fantasia* (Disney/1990R-50th Anniversary) 24.8
16. *Rescuers Down Under* (Disney/1990) 23.7
17. *The Fox And The Hound* (Disney/1988R) 23.6
18. *The Jungle Book* (Disney/1984R) 23.0
19. *The Care Bears Movie* (Nelvana/1985) 22.9
20. *The Black Cauldron* (Disney/1985) 21.3

Of the top ten, eight are Disney's. The other two feature Steven Spielberg's name above the title. All but three have been released on home video.

What made these cartoons cash machines? Let's look at the top ten. For each there's a small synopsis and a little background into the history/development of the film. Finally, since most have come out on video (and the other three may join them), there are a pair of reviews: for those who have become so used to movie review teams that a single review is not enough perspective. Now play producer and try to figure out what would be the best new idea for an animated feature.

The Little Mermaid (1989) was Disney's return to classic fairy tales as a basis for their features. The story, based on a Hans Christian Anderson tale, follows Ariel, a mermaid who falls in love with a human. She visits the sea witch in order to exchange her fins for legs so that she can try to win his love. The film was written

*Above:
Trade ad
heralding ticket
sales for The
Land Before
Time.
©1988 Sullivan
Bluth*

and directed by John Musker and Ron Clements. The Oscar winning score was by Howard Ashman and Alan Menken. This feature was one of Disney's strongest in decades. It was loved by critics and audiences alike. It's score, a reggae/Jamaican style, was equally successful, winning numerous awards and a gold album. Musker and Clements had worked together on *The Great Mouse Detective* (1986) and continued their desire for strong story. In fact, *Mermaid* was one of the first Disney features to be developed from a script (by Musker and

How To Make A Hit Animated Feature

Above:
Ariel and friends.
© Walt Disney Company

Clements), and not an outline and presentation art, as most Disney features were. When released on home video, the tape sold over nine million, becoming one of the top selling cassettes in history. Disney has mentioned a sequel.

Cawley: Easily one of the best written animated films of the decade. It's hard to dislike a film where the characters are pleasant, the songs are fun and the animation is generally excellent. However, there is a definite sterile quality to the picture. There are no surprises, no experiments, no flash. It is a perfect example of a "typical" Disney feature.

Korkis: This bright and fast moving film charmed audiences so completely that few ever questioned story gaps like how the main menace was so easily dispatched. The story of a young girl's rapid maturity when faced with adversity was in many ways a re-telling of Disney's *Pinocchio* with the crab substituting for Jiminy Cricket. Ariel was sexier than previous Disney heroines and the art style for the film was a clear break from previous Disney features and made it worth repeated viewings.

Oliver & Company (1988) was the first Disney feature produced totally under the Eisner regime. It is also one their "hippest" since *Jungle Book*. The film is an extremely loose re-telling of Dickens' Oliver Twist with dogs. Oliver, a kitten, is taken in by a band of dogs, led by Dodger, who steal for their owner. When Oliver is adopted by a nice girl, Oliver's connection with the gang puts the girl in jeopardy. The film debuted with only mild publicity due to Disney's publicity department still working overtime on *Who Framed Roger Rabbit?* It did receive generally favorable reviews with critics pointing out its upbeat feel and fine voice work (including Billy Joel and Bette Midler). However it initially failed to perform at the box office as well as *The Land Before Time* (released the same day). After a few weeks, though it soon took off and was quickly beating *Land* on a week-to-week basis to eventually triumph. Some of the press did notice that the film did not look very good. Though directed by George Scribner, many insiders state it was the intervention (after a year of work on the film without a completed story) of executive Jeffrey Katzenburg who got the project on track and made it so "hip."

Korkis: While the fast pace of *Oliver* hides flaws, later reflection about the film is disturbing. Many people, including film critics, didn't realize that Oliver was a cat, probably because he is overshadowed by the other more extreme characters who don't effectively interact with each other. Rather than a story, the film is a series of visually dramatic sequences that throws story logic to the wind.

Cawley: The film was fun and lively for the most part. It did contain some of the weakest drawing seen in a Disney feature as well as generally flat, uninspired character designs. Lively voice work and fast cutting helped to cover up most of the poor story work. It, no doubt, due to its success, will be another model for future Disney (and other studio) features.

Snow White (1937) Disney's first feature is always a money maker. Few are unaware of the story behind "Disney's Folly" in which everyone was certain that an animated feature would be a box office disaster. However, when the film opened it became the highest grossing film in motion picture history! (A record it held until the release of *Gone With The Wind*.) The well-known and oft-copied tale, is about a princess (Snow White) who must hide in the woods from her wicked stepmother who's a witch. In 1987 the film was released on its 50th anniversary. It opened in more theaters on one day than any film (animated or otherwise) in history with a great deal of hoopla. For this special release, the film became the first of the Disney classics to be "shaved" at the top and bottom to accommodate modern screen sizes. (Disney has now made it a policy

that all pre-1955 features will receive this treatment when re-issued.) It also featured a high priced opening day ticket that included a special medallion. Many movie industry watchers thought this was a clever gimmick. When Disney repeated the higher-price-with-souvenir gimmick on *Dick Tracy*, the

Below:
Littlefoot in The Land Before Time.
©1988
Universal City
Studios

same observers thought it was a cheap way of getting a higher opening gross!

Cawley: Story, voice, art and music all come together into a well crafted movie. In fact, this film is one of the better musicals of all time. (It even pre-dates *Oklahoma* in using songs to convey story points.) However, like many

KEEP HAIR, THAT RADIATES FROM FIEVEL'S HEAD, "SPIKEY."

BOTTOM EDGE OF TUNIC HAS A RAGGED LOOK:

SMALL ROLLED CUFFS

HI-LITE ON CAPS VISOR.

KEEP PANT'S CROTCH LOW.

classics it is truly representative of its time and now shows signs of being dated. Using it as a base for future films is a mistake.

Korkis: It is amazing how effective this film still is despite the handicaps of an irritating voice for the heroine and a cloying approach to romance. It is like an old European fairy tale picture book come to life with characters more fully realized than some of their live action contemporaries and a satisfyingly emotional story.

The Land Before Time (1987) For Spielberg's second feature with Don Bluth, he went back to basics and back in time. The film's story follows Littlefoot, a brontosaurus, who teams with other young dinosaurs in a trek to find a mysterious valley. Originally conceived as a *Bambi* in prehistoric times, Spielberg planned for

Above:
Model sheet
drawings of
Fievel.
© 1984 Don Bluth

the film to have no dialogue and, like the "Rites of Spring" sequence in *Fantasia*, be an epic adventure. The story shifted as time progressed and a new member of the Spielberg/Bluth team arrived (George Lucas). Once again backed by a powerful publicity and merchandising drive, *Land* opened to make history as the highest grossing opening weekend in animation history. Despite mostly poor reviews, the film did well for the first few weeks. However word of mouth or the lack of desire for repeated viewing found the film beginning to drop off. Prior to the film's release, Spielberg cut around 15 minutes out of the film that he found "too intense" for children. In several interviews, director Don Bluth expressed dissatisfaction with Spielberg's handling of the film. This was the first film

done in Ireland by Sullivan-Bluth Studios.

Korkis: Didn't the public realize that even if the dinosaurs reached the valley they were all going to die shortly anyway? The film tries for a mystical, lyrical approach that is not supported by the story nor the precious protagonists. Unfortunately, this attempt is a huge disappointment to dinosaur fans and animation fans who didn't need a watered down version of *Bambi* with scales.

Cawley: Even at its edited length, this film was incredibly dull. Once again, story was sacrificed for cute characters and "classical" animation. The work on the adult dinosaurs was subtle and impressive, but the young crew suffered due to "cute" voices and design (they all have eyelashes). It's a shame that the men who took fantasy films out of the "kiddie matinee" arena seem intent on dragging animation deeper into "for kids only."

An American Tail (1986) was the first animated feature to come from Spielberg, king of cinema blockbusters. The story followed Fievel, a Russian-Jewish mouse, on his trip to America in which he becomes separated from his family. It was directed by Don Bluth (*The Secret of Nimh/Dragon's Lair*), and produced by Sullivan-Bluth Studios (now in Ireland; in fact, the inking and painting of the film was largely done in Ireland). Not based on any well known characters, the film did boast one of the biggest merchandising and publicity blitzes seen in animation history. Sears and other companies were brought in at the beginning to assist in the design of characters to ensure proper marketability and popularity. The story, slightly inspired by Spielberg's grandfather (who was also called Fievel), told of Russian mice emigrating to the U.S. The film initially received mild to negative critical reaction, but "Fievel-mania" hit and the film went on to become a major success becoming the first non-Disney animated feature to break Disney's box-office records and becoming the highest grossing animated feature on first release. It later went to

videotape where it was number two in sales for almost a year. Spielberg produced a sequel to the film without Don Bluth.

Cawley: Despite the success of the film, I dislike it. The story is fragmented and misdirected. Characters are unattractive, with some of the worst voice work (most notably the whiny Fievel) since Saturday Morning of the Seventies. If you take away the fluid (and often overdone) animation this film has all the markings of a bad Care Bears feature.

Korkis: An unfocused story with a host of unmemorable characters lost in over-animation. Obviously something about being lost or separated struck a strong chord in the American public and has given this film more success than it deserves. Especially irritating are the false climaxes where Fievel is almost reunited with his family.

The Jungle Book (original release 1967) is the only feature to make the top twenty twice! Its 1990 reissue logged in at number six, while the 1984 reissue hit number 18. (*The Fox And The Hound*'s original release appears in the top 25, while an earlier reissue of *Fantasia* came in at number 33.) The film, based on stories by Rudyard Kipling, followed a mancub (Mowgli) raised by wolves. When Shere Kahn (a tiger) returns, Mowgli is

forced to journey to the man village. On the way he meets Baloo (a bear). The last feature fully supervised by Walt Disney, the film became one of the studios top grossing features on first release. The score (largely by the Sherman Brothers who wrote *Mary Poppins* and others) was breezy. Key to the film's success was Phil Harris' interpretation of Baloo and the show stopping "The Bear Necessities" song (by Terry Gilkyson). Harris' Baloo became the basis for the *Tale Spin* series from Disney TV, which has nothing to do with the film. (Harris doesn't supply the voice for TV.)

Korkis: The last animated feature supervised by Walt himself, this film was a disappointment on its first release but looks remarkably better today when compared with recent offerings. Some animation was borrowed from a previous Disney short, *Goliath II* (1960). There are individual scenes that are outstanding surrounding a story and a hero who are uninteresting and aimless. Phil Harris' voice work was so distinctive it is difficult to imagine anyone else doing the character.

Cawley: A flawed gem. The story wanders at times and the animation is occasionally inconsistent. However, this is a perfect example of a star "saving" the show. Phil Harris' Baloo

How To Make A Hit Animated Feature

makes all the nonsense work and is a joy to watch. Though the animation is not as rich as the Disney "classics," it is still in full control, exhibiting full personalities without the need for extreme exaggeration and takes now accepted as "full animation."

Bambi (original release - 1942) One of the most serious animated features by Disney, the film was not successful in its first release. Based on Felix Salten's novel, the story follows the life of a deer (Bambi) from birth, to first love, to children of his own. (Yes, Bambi is a male.) Famous for the creation of Thumper (not in the book by Salten) and the death of Bambi's mother, *Bambi* is also one of Disney's simpler films. The story is simply a short biography of a deer in the forest. Oddly the film has become more and more controversial with each reissue. Its grim look at forest life and man's intrusion has become commonly criticized by those advocating hunting and those advocating less violence in children's films. Of more recent debate is the question of sex discrimination. Some critics now claim the view of females in the film is the epitome of Disney's male dominated universe. They cite the romance sequence as key to the problem as the female creatures are shown

Below:
Story sketch from Bambi.
©1952 Walt Disney Productions

to be merely interested in getting a male and unable to protect themselves. Though both aspects (anti-hunting and animal mating rituals) are based on facts, the critics seem to agree that neither has a place in a film aimed at children.

Cawley: One of my favorite animated features, and one of my top ten features of all time. A simple tale, told elegantly and with little dialogue. The musical score is rich, and the songs, though dated, still add mood. The Disney artists never had better command of the true art of animation, when it meant acting and feeling through subtle movement, gestures and attitude rather than continual motion.

Korkis: This film truly reflects Walt Disney's desire to have animation imitate life rather than strive to achieve things only possible in animation and in my opinion Disney animated features suffered because of this. The well regarded emotional moments in this film pale in comparison to similar moments in *Dumbo*. When people talk about cute Disney animals, this is one of the first films that spring to my mind.

Cinderella (original release - 1951) This was Disney's first full length feature after World War II (following a string of compilation films such as *Three Caballeros, Melody Time*

and *Ichabod And Mr. Toad*). It was also his first major box-office success in many years. The story is based on Perrault's tale of a pretty girl relegated to cleaning and slaving by her evil stepmother. All seems lost until Cinderella's fairy godmother appears. Relying on the fairy tale musical premise, Disney again found critical and audience satisfaction. When recently released to home video, it became the top selling tape in history (until the release of *E.T.*), selling over 7 million copies.

Korkis: While the film has a handful of memorable sequences, it pales next to *Sleeping Beauty* which has a similar storyline. Without the comedy support of the mice, the lead characters would be unable to sustain interest in the story. The rotoscoped humans seem to distance an audience from the film, despite the claim that one of Walt's all time favorite animated sequences was Cinderella getting her ball gown.

Cawley: Definitely a classic and one of Disney's best written films. However, the feature still leaves me a bit cold. Perhaps the "Cinderella" myth holds no fascination for me, or that the characters, though well developed don't interest me.

101 Dalmatians (original release 1961) told the bright story (based on a book by Dodie Smith) of a Dalmatian

and his owner (the story is told from the dog's perspective) who find romance. The harmony is broken, though, when Cruella DeVille plans to use the Dalmatians' new puppies for a coat. This was Disney's first feature to showcase the Xerox process (in lieu of inking). It was also a break from his earlier fantasy/ period pieces as the story took place in recent times. (In fact the disappointing box office of *Sleeping Beauty* made Disney state that it was obvious fairy tales were no longer of interest to modern audiences and that the only reason re-issues of earlier films did well was because of the recognition and nostalgia factors.) The film had an art nouveau look with a breezy style. Another "dog" film, this one proved a major success at the box office upon its first release. It also continued the line of songs in animated films, but even though the lead human was a song writer, the feature had no "musical numbers."

Cawley: A fun feature that's light and breezy. However, unlike *Oliver*, this film has great character designs and a sharp story. Again, its one of the better written animated features with a direct story and keenly carved characters. I wish more animation studios and students would study this film than *Pinocchio*.

Korkis: No one can watch this film without

whistling the theme song of Cruella deVille, one of the most memorable characters in animation. The story elements are logical and the suspense builds naturally. Despite its more modern style of drawing, the film has a timeless quality about it but it has never received the accolades it deserves.

Lady And The Tramp (original release 1955) Disney's first "dog" film and one of his most popular features. The typical story of a rich, society girl's romance with a man from the "wrong side" of the tracks is given a canine twist. The first animated feature released in Cinemascope, the film proved successful with

critics (generally) and the audience. Another "break" from his string of fairy tales, *Lady* was based almost entirely on in-house development. (An early version sans Tramp appears in the 1941 book Walt Disney's Surprise Package.) The film, for the first time in a Disney feature showed the direct relationship between humans and their pets and/ or animals (to be seen again in *101 Dalmatians, Aristocats, Rescuers, Great Mouse Detective* and *Oliver*). When released on home video, it became the best selling title in history (until the release, one year later, of *Cinderella*). Peggy Lee, who wrote the songs and provided the voice of Peg (who sings "He's a Tramp"), successfully sued Disney over the home video version. She alleged that her contract gave her control over selling recorded versions of her songs, all found in the videotape.

Korkis: One of my all time favorite Disney films that showcases distinctive, interesting characters that are easy to care about and a story that offers subtle humor and suspense missing from modern animated films. Truly one of the great romantic films that deals with the subject in an amazingly mature fashion.

Cawley: Another favorite of mine. Once again it shows Disney artists doing what they do best. The writing is

not as strong as other features (some sequences seem more in tune with the need for songs or comedy than story). However the romance scenes between Lady and Tramp are some of the most memorable in screen history. Anyone who has seen the film will not forget their dinner in the alley behind an Italian restaurant.

Were you able to find the magic common denominator that made these films a hit? Some think they did. Features announced to appear in the early part of the Nineties included: *Rock-A-Doodle* (a rock and roll re-telling of the Chanticleer legend of a rooster who thinks his crowing brings up the sun), *Aladdin* (a musical based on the classic story of the genie in the lamp), *Freddi As F.R.0.7.* (a frog as an international spy), *Tom & Jerry: The Movie* (starring the famous cat and mouse team, this time as friends and talking), and *Rover Dangerfield* (comedian Rodney Dangerfield as a dog).

How will the public react to these new films? All are hoping to find a spot on the top ten. If they do, no doubt the considered formula for a hit will be altered to accommodate the newcomer's style.

Below: Original release ad for number ten. © Walt Disney Productions

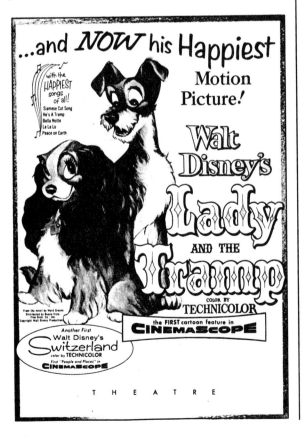

Spine-tingling adventure
and fun with an all-time
monster favorite and his
comical, cowardly cousin

Hanna-Barbera Enterprises, Inc.

CHAPTER TEN:

ANIMONSTERS

TOP SECRET

"Monsters lead such interesting lives" according to Bugs Bunny in *Hair Raising Hare* (1946). This favorite short has Bugs pretend to be a beauty shop manicurist in order to fool a huge, hairy, orange, sneaker-wearing monster (now known as Gossamer).

Monsters do indeed have interesting lives and the

Below: Concept drawing from 1980 for an unproduced Daffy Duck short. © 1980 Warner Brothers

DUCKULA

more popular and famous the monster, the more interesting and varied a life it will have. Since the beginning of storytelling, monsters have played a large part in our lives. From the evil forces of mythology to Gothic novels to the movie screens TV screens and comic books, audiences continue to have a deep affection and fascination for these creatures. Wolfmen, vampires, mummies, zombies, atomic mutations, creatures from space and supernatural creations have happily terrorized us.

In 1973, *The Monster Times*, a newspaper devoted to fantasy films, conducted a poll to determine the favorite classic monsters. According to the readers, the top four favorites were Godzilla, Dracula, Frankenstein and King Kong. These four characters are perfect examples of four key types of monsters.

Dracula and Frankenstein showcase man as the monster with the former being a dead man becoming an "undead" horror, while the latter highlights a menace created by man. Both are also based on Gothic fiction. Godzilla and King Kong focus on giant, natural terrors with the first being a kind of revenge of nature, the latter nature gone wild. These two were original creations for the movie screen.

These popular classics

have had a long and interesting career in the world of cinema. They have also proved somewhat perennial animated personalities.

The Classics

Like so many popular characters in fiction, it took motion pictures to make international stars out of Frankenstein and Dracula. The initial reaction to these films in the early Thirties is hard to believe today. A double bill of these two films often required that doctors, nurses and ambulances be available outside a theater for the stricken patrons overcome by the horror of it all. The strong imagery found in these early films proved indelible enough to become a permanent part of our visual culture.

The word "Frankenstein" conjures up images of a giant, inarticulate Boris Karloff in heavy makeup; a heavy, lumbering walk; electrodes sticking out of his neck; and a slightly flattened head. This look is actually trademarked by Universal Pictures, producer of the first films. In the original book Frankenstein was the doctor's name and his creation was known only as "the monster." Such is the power of film that today, the monster, itself, is known throughout the world as Frankenstein.

Due to the lack of such heavy make-up, the image of Dracula is a bit less

Left:
Frankenstone
animation
drawing.
© Hanna-Barbera

distinctive. Bela Lugosi played the infamous Count in Universal's original *Dracula*. Most viewers remember for the long flowing black cape, the staring eyes, and the change into a bat (done via animation). Though Count Dracula is a definite character, unlike Frankenstein's monster he is not totally unique. He is merely a vampire, one of allegedly many.

As stated earlier, these films were taken very seriously when first released. Cartoons, though, were a different matter. Such easily identifiable personalities were open game for the caricaturing cartoonists. Just as Clark Gable, W.C. Fields, Shirley Temple, Douglas Fairbanks and other cinema stars would appear as cartoon cameos, so would the classic Universal creations. In these animated moments, the monsters frequently appeared together. (By the late Thirties, Universal followed animations lead and began placing their monsters together in such films as *The House Of Dracula*.)

One of the first animated appearances the Frankenstein monster and Dracula made was in *Mickey's Gala Premier* (1933). They attend the opening of a new Mickey Mouse cartoon along with other celebrities. Most of the other studios were just as quick to jump on the Frankenstein band wagon.

At Warners, the villain in *Porky's Road Race* (1937) is Borax Karloff, a combination of a mad scientist and the famous monster. Two years later, a cowardly Frankenstein would put in a brief appearance in *Porky's Movie Mystery* (1939). That same year, a truly frightening Frankenstein appeared in *Sniffles And The Bookworm*.

Even Bugs Bunny got into the act, imitating Karloff as the monster in *What's Cookin' Doc* (1944) and being a "Frankicense monster" briefly in *Hare Conditioned* (1945). In the 1960 Warners cartoon *Transylvania 6-5000,* a Count Dracula-type vampire, named Count Bloodcount, tried unsuccessfully to turn Bugs Bunny into a vampire.

Terrytoons had *Frankenstein's Cat* (1942) where Mighty Mouse (then known as Super Mouse) had to battle the doctor's pet cat who had kidnapped a bird. In *The Ghost Town* (1944), a vampire bat leads a Frankenstein monster while Gandy Goose watches intently. *The Jailbreak* (1946), another Mighty Mouse cartoon, revealed that Frankenstein and Dracula were prisoners at Alcatraz prison. Frankenstein even lumbered about in *King Tut's*

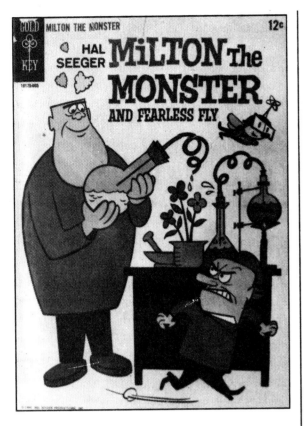

Tomb (1950) with Heckle and Jeckle.

Woody Woodpecker ran into a mad scientist in *Monster Of Ceremonies*(1966) where he was transformed into a Frankenstein Woodpecker and *Magoo Meets Frankenstein*(1960) pitted the near sighted Mr. Magoo against Professor Frankenstein who had transferred the intelligence of a chicken into the head of the monster. One of Dracula's most unusual and generally forgotten appearances was in *Batula* (1952) a puppet short which also featured Al Capp's Fearless Fosdick!

By the late Fifties and early Sixties, the showing of the early Universal horror films on TV made the monsters accessible to a new younger audience. This same generation watched the real monsters side by side with their cartoon counterparts (due to the cartoons also being shown on TV). No longer truly terrifying, the monsters had shifted into trendy, sometimes campy, characters.

A Frankenstein inspired animated hero was Milton the Monster who originally appeared in 1965. Professor Weirdo had put too many drops of tenderness into his creation and ended up with a monster who sounded like Gomer Pyle and was lovable. Milton had a flat head from which he could occasionally blow puffs of smoke.

One attempt to tell a serious version of the Frankenstein story in animation was an episode of *The Famous Adventures Of Mr. Magoo* (1965) where Magoo played the scientist attempting to conquer the world with his creation. The half hour format, like other adaptations, corrupted and distorted the original story.

On September 10, 1966, *Frankenstein Jr. And The Impossibles* premiered on Saturday morning TV. Frankenstein Jr. was a huge robot who could fly and think. He was controlled by Buzz Conroy, a young boy whose father was a famous scientist. Frankenstein Jr.

was a typical superhero. He had a cape and a mask. The robot was activated by a radar ring worn by Buzz. Each week they would zoom out of a mountain top laboratory to battle evil like Spider Man and the Alien Brain from outer space. Created by Hanna-Barbera, Frankenstein Jr's voice was credited to Ted Cassidy, who portrayed Lurch the butler on *The Addams Family* TV Show.

The real (Doctor) Frankenstein appeared in the puppet animated feature film *Mad Monster Party* (1966). (The models were designed by famed Mad Magazine cartoonist Jack Davis.) In the film, Baron Von Frankenstein invites his nephew and all the classic monsters to his castle for a special announcement. Dracula played the villain, trying to turn the rest of the monsters against the Baron.

A cel animated sequel, *The Mad Mad Monsters* (1972) was a Saturday Superstar Movie for ABC. Once again, Baron Von Frankenstein invites the classic monsters to a special wedding at the Transylvania Astoria. This time it is for the wedding of the Frankenstein monster. Dracula not only shows up, but with a son named Boobula. Both these films were produced by Rankin-Bass.

A lovable Frankenstein (called "Frankie) and Dracula appeared in *The*

0168-9000

© HANNA-BARBERA PRODUCTIONS INC. 1990

MONSTER TAILS

MAIN MODELS

MAR 13 1990

15

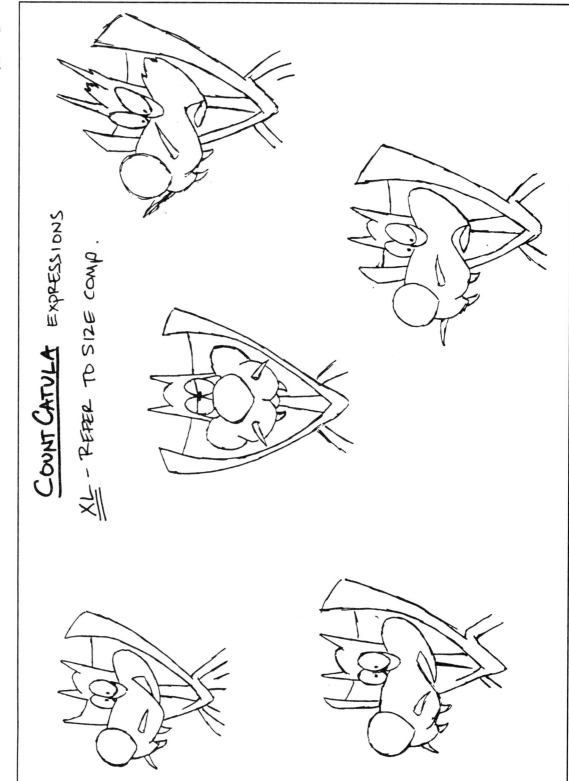

COUNT CATULA EXPRESSIONS

XL - REFER TO SIZE COMP.

Groovie Goolies from Filmation in 1970. The show was a sort of variety-musical comedy format with lots of blackout gags. Dracula was played for laughs in the *Groovie Goolies*. Sometimes the Count would change from bat to man in mid-air and end up crashing to the ground. Often times, storylines revolved around Sabrina the Teen-Age Witch trying to hide these relatives from her friends. When the show premiered on CBS, a rock group called the *Groovie Goolies* performed at such

Below:
Record album featuring the live action and animated Goolies.
© Filmation

places as Los Angeles' Magic Castle to plug the show. The *Goolies* last appearance was in a 1972 *Saturday Superstar Movie* from Filmation entitled *Porky Pig and Daffy Duck Meet the Groovie Goolies*. The *Goolies* had to save the famous Warner Brothers stars from a Phantom of the Opera inspired character who was terrorizing a movie

studio. At the end of the cartoon, the *Goolies* burst forth into the real world as flesh and blood characters.

An unusual twist on the classic monsters was the 1980 Hanna-Barbera series, *Drak Pack*. Three teenage boys, who were related to the classic monsters, could transform themselves into Dracula, Frankenstein and the Werewolf to do good deeds to atone for the evil of their ancestors. Drak Jr., Frankie and Howler got their orders from Big D (great grandfather Dracula) to go out and fight O.G.R.E. (*Organization of Generally Rotten Enterprises*). The teenage boys could transform by clasping their right hands together and yelling the word "wacko!"

Frankenstein (or Frankenstein inspired themes) and Dracula (or similarly dressed vampires) have been featured on countless animated series including *Popeye*, *Scooby-Doo*, *Super Chicken*, *Underdog*, the *Three Stooges*, and *The Funny Company*. They've also made occasional animated appearances in features.

In *Yellow Submarine* (1968) Beatle Ringo Starr enters a laboratory where he finds the Frankenstein Monster lying on a platform. Using the electrical equipment he brings the monster to life and it changes into Beatle Lennon. The title sequence for *Return of the Pink Panther* (1975),

animated by the Richard William's studio, feature the Panther imitating the monster. The mid-seventies also found a serious animated production of Dracula produced in Japan as a TV-movie. The film, based on the Marvel comics series of the time, as scheduled to be released in the U.S., but never was.

In the Eighties, both Frankenstein and Dracula have become the basis for Frankenberry and Count Chocula cereals animated commercials. *The Mini-Monsters*, part of *The Comic Strip* (1987) syndicated series from Rankin-Bass, based the monsters' children at a summer camp. The "original" monsters appeared in one of the first animated theatrical shorts made by Warner Brothers after 20 years of inactivity, *Night Of The Living Duck* (1988). In it, Daffy Duck croons the song "Monsters Lead Such Interesting Lives."

Other recent variations included the Cosgrove-Hall series *Count Duckula* about a vampire duck (originally a villain on their *Dangermouse* series). In 1990, Hanna-Barbera offered *Monster Tails*, part of the *Wake, Rattle & Roll* series. *Tails* tells the story of the monster's pets, designed by comic artist Don Dougherty, left at home while the monsters head off to Hollywood.

The Giants.
One of the most durable

and famous monsters of all time is the mighty giant ape, *King Kong*. he is also one of the first monster superstars created specifically for the silver screen. Unlike some monster friends, King Kong actually began as an animated character! His first appearance in 1933 was animated by stop motion pioneer Willis O'Brien.

King Kong was in its first year of release when it began being spoofed in animated cartoons. *King Klunk* was a Universal short featuring the Walter Lantz character, Pooch the Pup. Pooch goes to a lost island with his girlfriend where they discover a giant ape. King Klunk falls in love with Pooch's girlfriend and even battles a dinosaur that threatens her. The ape is brought back to New York where he duplicates Kong's demise.

Also, in 1933, Walt Disney released a Mickey Mouse short entitled *The Pet Store*. At Mickey's pet shop, a caged gorilla falls in love with Minnie Mouse, breaks free and carries her to the top of a bird cage where he is defeated by Mickey and a flock of birds in a scene very suggestive of the film it was parodying. That same year at Warner Brothers, they released *I Like Mountain Music* (animated by Friz Freleng) where characters on magazine covers come to life. The hero is "Ping Pong" a giant gorilla from the cover

of *Screenplay* magazine who comes to life just in time to trap the bad guys. Even Willis O'Brien returned to Kong that year with the release of the sequel, *Son Of Kong* (1933).

Giant gorillas, always popular as a menace, now took King Kong attitudes with one springing off a box of animal crackers in Warner Brothers *Goofy Groceries* (1940). Another terrorized Superman in *Terror on the Midway* (1941). The homage continued to more modern cartoon series like *Underdog* where the super pup must rescue Sweet Polly from the hairy paws of yet another King Kong clone.

Hanna-Barbera tried to make a huge purple ape into a lovable monster in their 1975 series featuring the Great Grape Ape. This huge simian was incredibly stupid but tremendously good hearted. He needed guidance from his dog companion, Beegle Beagle. In one

*Above:
Record album
featuring the
animated Kong.*

*Below
King Kong and
friends.
Both © 1991
Rankin-Bass*

episode, Grape Ape even had to rescue an actress from the clutches of Tonzilla.

However, Kong's best remembered brush with cel animation was *The King Kong Show* which premiered Saturday morning on ABC on September 10, 1966. Produced by Rankin-Bass, this series was one of the first animated in Japan for U.S. network presentation. Ignoring Kong's death plunge from the Empire State Building over three decades earlier, this series revealed that Kong was living happily on Mondo Island located in the Java Sea.

A U.S. family stumbles across the friendly ape when the father, Professor Bond, establishes a research center on the island. His young son, Bobby, and his daughter, Susan, befriend the gorilla

just in time to use his tremendous size and strength to battle a horde of menaces that threaten them and the world during their only season of episodes. One recurring villain was the nasty Dr. Who (no relation to the popular British television science fiction character), a mad scientist who sought to control the mighty Kong for dastardly deeds. (Curiously, Dr. Who was the main villain in the live action *King Kong Escapes* film made by Toho in 1967. In the film, Dr. Who uses a huge robot dubbed "Mechani-Kong" until he is able to drug and capture the real ape.)

The official ABC press release for the program described Kong as "a lovable ape." The release also promised that during the series, Kong would "perform awesome, sometimes earth-shaking deeds to bring evildoers to justice."

ABC decided to introduce the show with a hour-long prime time special on September 6, 1966 titled simply *King Kong*. Basically it was two half hour episodes from the regular show combined into one story. The Bonds discover Kong who battles an enormous monster from the sea know as the Kraken. They bring Kong to New York where he climbs the Empire State Building but instead of being shot by planes, merely climbs back down to rejoin the Bond family. This special was the first preview of a Saturday morning show aired in prime time on ABC. (The previous year, NBC had aired an hour long special entitled *The World of Secret Squirrel and Atom Ant* using segments from the then upcoming new *SatAM* show.)

Homage to King Kong continued over the years in cel animation including cameos in later animated efforts like *Yellow Submarine* (1968) and the titles of *The Pink Panther Strikes Again* (1976). Kong himself appeared several times in live action, such as the aforementioned *King Kong Escapes* and the earlier *King Kong vs Godzilla* (1962). However in these films he was portrayed by a man in a costume, not stop motion animation.

In 1975, Michael Eisner saw Bette Midler do a King Kong spoof in her musical show "*Clams on the Half Shell*" and thought it would be a great idea to do a rock musical version of King Kong with Midler playing the Fay Way part. Eisner, then with ABC, talked with both Universal and Paramount about the project. The result was that both Paramount and Universal announced competing Kong films. (Only Paramount's was made.) Due to the controversy on Kong's ownership, in September, 1976, there was a court ruling that the novelization of King Kong was in public domain.

December 1, 1976, Fred Calvert, then president of Farmhouse Films announced that he was preparing a six part mini-series of King Kong for Saturday morning. This was nearly a year before the ratings smash of *Roots* would make the mini-series format so popular in prime time. The project never developed any further. (Calvert's next series was the Saturday morning *I Am The Greatest: The Adventures Of Muhammad Ali* on NBC in 1977 featuring the voice of Ali.)

December 23, 1976 it was announced that DePatie-Freleng, well known for their work with the Pink Panther series, had joined with producers Walter Bien and Gene Farmer to develope a Saturday morning TV series based on the classic story of King Kong. Like many such development projects, it quietly disappeared. Since that time, Kong has been largely relegated to live action features and TV commercials.

One of his rare modern cameos occurred in a 1990 episode of *Alvin and the Chipmunks Go To The Movies*. In it, Kong lives in the jungle with his companion Theodore when both are brought back to civilization by Alvin, playing an unscrupulous promoter.

Almost as popular as Kong is the Japanese

Left:
Promotional flyer
for Hanna-
Barbera's
Godzilla.
©1978
Hanna-Barbera
Productions

monster, Godzilla. *Godzilla, King of the Monsters* was released in the United States in 1956. The effects creator of Godzilla, Eiji Tsuburaya, had been a fan of *King Kong* and wanted to create a modern version of the "giant monster" theme. Unlike Kong, the film did not feature stop motion animation but a man in a foam rubber reptile suit.

Godzilla became a major hit and a series of sequels soon began starring a "second" Godzilla (since the first had been totally atomized in the original). Initially these sequels continued the theme of him being a terrorizing monster. By the mid-sixties, though, his image began to change. Suddenly Godzilla found himself living on Monster island and saving the earth from giant robots and alien invaders. Because of these later films where he fought everything from *"the Thing"* to *"the Smog Monster,"* Godzilla became the icon for the "Japanese monster movie" which often meant silly monsters and less than adequate effects.

Godzilla's image was parodied in a number of animated efforts including the *Flinstones* ("Rockzilla") and *Frankenstein Jr.* ("Gadzooka"). One of the most memorable parodies was Marv Newland's infamous *Bambi Meets Godzilla* (1969). In this 30 second short, Disney's Bambi is seen grazing as a long list of credits roll by the action. Just as the credits finish, Godzilla's huge hind foot squashes the gentle deer flat against the ground. A little know sequel, *Bambi's Revenge,* appeared many years later. In it, Bambi uses a bazooka to blow Godzilla's foot to pieces.

Like King Kong, Godzilla tried Saturday morning. Henry Saperstein, president of UPA (who was responsible for Mr. Magoo) owned the U.S. rights to the character and tried to get NBC interested in a straight adaptation. It was Joe Barbera of Hanna-Barbera who suggested using Godzilla as a cartoon hero. (He was already a live action film hero.) On september 1978, *The Godzilla Power Hour* debuted with a half hour Godzilla segment and a half hour devoted to Jana, a blond female Tarzan-like character who lived in the Amazon Jungle.

In the Godzilla stories, Captain Carl Majors commanded the research ship "Calico," inspired by Jacques Cousteau's "Calypso." His crew was able to rescue Godzooky, a cousin of Godzilla.

Godzooky was a diminutive, flying green, dragon who had a puppy dog eagerness. His voice was supplied by Don Messick, best know as the voice of Scooby-Doo. Reportedly, Godzooky was the creation of comic artist Doug Wildey (who was also largely responsible for Jonny Quest). Godzilla's rumblings were provided by Ted Cassidy, famous as Lurch the butler on the *Addams Family*.

In gratitude, Godzilla became a friend of the research vessel and Captain majors could summon the beast from the watery depths by pressing a button on his hand-held electronic signaller. Godzilla could not only breath fire, but was able to emit laser beams from his eyes to help defeat such menaces as the Seaweed Monster, The Colossus of Atlantis, The Time Dragon and the Eartheater. Only thirteen Godzilla episodes where made.

Interestingly, the first designs by Hanna-Barbera for Godzilla were rejected by Toho because Godzilla's face did not look "apelike" enough. Godzilla's Japanese name was "Gojira" which was taken from the U.S. word for "gorilla" (due to the Kong influence) and the Japanese word for whale, "kujira." Hanna-Barbara's artists had tried to make Godzilla look more like a dinosaur or reptilian dragon. The face was changed to be more apelike and was finally approved.

Like his giant prototype, Godzilla has been largely unanimated for some time, relying more on live action features starring rubber suited actors. An attempt in the Eighties to return to the original, terrifying Godzilla did not prove successful. However, the old "friendly" Godzilla films continue as popular camp.

Monsters still lead interesting lives. The classic monsters have become part of our culture. Toys, costumes, trading cards, T-shirts, comic books, bubble baths and countless other merchandising items have featured these beasts and have captured the hearts and pocketbooks of children of all ages. the world of animation was just another of the many areas where monsters roamed successfully over the years. No matter how thoroughly they were disposed of at the end of each film, audiences demanded these horrors be resurrected for further adventures. Even today the indestructible classic monsters merely await some enterprising animation studio to once again unleash them on an unsuspecting world.

Right: Godzilla's cameo in Bambi Meets Godzilla. © Marv Newland

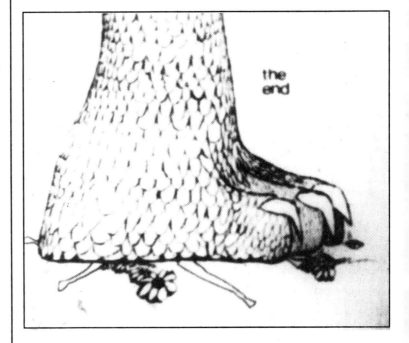

TOP SECRET

CHAPTER ELEVEN:

BUY AND CEL: HISTORY AND GUIDE TO ANIMATION ART COLLECTING

In 1989, a rare cel from *Orphan's Benefit* (1934), a Mickey Mouse cartoon, was sold in a $450,000 transaction. That sale topped a previous high price in 1988 for a cel and water color background of Mickey Mouse from *The Mad Doctor* (1933) which sold for almost $64,000.

A color tracing of a cartoon character on something that looks like a sheet of plastic can now cost more than what an average American worker would make in years at a nine-to-five job. Whether high prices make something fine art is a debatable question but animation art collecting has opened the pocketbooks of buyers.

Recently cels from *Snow White* and *Pinocchio* only sold for $28, 600 and $17, 600 respectively. Thousands of visitors to Disneyland in the Sixties only spent a couple of dollars to purchase similarly authentic cels from Disney feature films. A cel bought in the early Sixties for a couple of dollars could now fetch prices topping five thousand: an increase of almost 100,000%!

No longer a small nickel and dime hobby, a novice buyer definitely needs some basic information about the subject so he doesn't get burned by this hot trend. Today, animation art collecting can get expensive and recent news reports of high prices paid for cel art

Right:
The original line art and the cel created from it.
© Filmation

can be intimidating.

A cel, from celluloid, is the most popular animation collectible. They were originally made of nitrate, like early films. Nitrate proved too unstable (at times flammable), so movies turned to celluloid and cels to acetate.

In any animated production, thousands of cels are needed. Each second of film contains twenty-four frames, though there are rarely twenty-four separate drawings used. Cels were considered just another step in the process of animation, and a temporary one at that. Ink and paint artists would trace the original animator's drawings onto the cel and paint the back of the image.

In the early days of animation, it was quite common for studios to cut costs by "washing" the paint off of previously used cels and reusing them. One of Warner Brothers' director Chuck Jones' first jobs in the business was washing off cels. At Terrytoons in the Forties, cels cost about three cents apiece. Tommy Morrison, who was a storyman, the voice of Mighty Mouse and the head of the opaquing department, got paid a penny a cel to wash off pictures of Mighty Mouse and Heckle and Jeckle. Morrison soon found someone willing to wash two cels for a penny and made a profit of a half cent each on the countless Terrytoon cels now lost to collectors.

Disney took care to save the original animation drawings, which could be later used for reference or copying, but was not as concerned about its cels. As Disney Studio Archivist Dave Smith once said, "They only saved the drawings. After all, with that, they could always ink and paint a new cel."

According to rumors, during the filming of *Fantasia*, after a scene had been filmed, some artists spread the already photographed cels on the floor and used them as an improvised Slip-And-Slide for amusement.

At Disney, some cels were given away as gifts to visitors and friends. Often these were not the actual production cels but special presentation cels made by the Ink and Paint Department because the actual cels were damaged during filming or hard to locate. Employees also took cels home to give to their children to play with or put up as a colorful picture on the nursery wall or merely to have a sample of their work.

Unlike other collectables, like comic books or records or gum cards, animation artwork was never meant to be in the public's hands. Cels, in particular, were discards and even today there are dumpsters at animation studios that are still treasure chests of discarded animation art for a knowledgeable collector and scavenger. In 1990, there was much publicity given to valuable animation artwork that one studio claimed was stolen and the other party said he found in boxes out by the trash cans.

It was Disney who began the trend of releasing artwork for sale to the public. The first official selling of animation art began in 1938 when Guthrie Courvoisier entered into a

Right:
The front and back of an animation cel.
© Hanna-Barbera Productions

contract with Disney to sell original art from *Snow White And The Seven Dwarfs*. This artwork eventually included not only original cels but backgrounds, animation drawings and story sketches. These were sold in specially

prepared set-ups that included certificates and mats. The arrangement was so successful that by mid-1939, the Courvoisier Gallery in San Francisco was also selling artwork from several Disney shorts including *Ferdinand The Bull* and *Donald's Golf Game* among others. (After Disney success at marketing artwork in the late Thirties, Warners made a short lived and unsuccessful attempt to do the same.)

By the time of *Pinocchio* (1940), even a small number of multiplane shots on glass were released for sale. Courvoisier maintained his licensing arrangement with Disney until late 1946. Some of these items sold for as high as twenty-five dollars which was a considerable but not unreasonable sum in those days. Sale of the artwork ceased by the late Forties. Today, the Courvoisier artwork is highly sought after because of its history.

With the opening of Disneyland in California in 1955, Disney, itself, sold cels from its animated cartoons at the Art Corner. The Corner was located in the old Tomorrowland connected to the Art of Animation exhibit. For five dollars, it was possible to purchase authentic cels featuring popular Disney characters. Spinner racks featured cels from *101 Dalmatians* among other productions, each different and in its own cardboard mat with a seal on the back. A cel of Jiminy Cricket in a cardboard mat might be on a merchandise counter next to the flip books and how-to-draw books.

Around 1970, the Disney organization became aware that some dealers were re-selling this art for as high as a hundred dollars apiece so the inexpensive treasures were withdrawn from Disneyland. The Disney art program was established and beginning with *Robin Hood* (1973), the studio offered its cels through art galleries and its amusement parks. The minimum retail price at that time was roughly sixty dollars a cel.

An exhibition of Disney animation art in 1981 at the Whitney Museum in New York sparked public interest in obtaining cels but it wasn't until 1984 that the first major auction devoted solely to selling animation art was held at Christies East. By the start of the Nineties such auctions were common across the country. Big time financial giants such as Steven Spielberg, George Lucas and Michael Jackson among others helped prices skyrocket. The prices on Disney's newer cels began to go up until the minimum

was around eighty dollars by the late Eighties.

Oddly, Disney was not in control of the prices of their artwork. Though the cels at the Parks had retail prices, all galleries and dealers paid a basic flat rate for cels from the Disney art program. The studio did not place a retail price for art. This concept began to change when the studio, under the newer management of Michael Eisner and Frank Wells became aware of how much money animation artwork was now worth.

The studio brought in two top Disney merchandisers, Bruce Hamilton and Russ Cochran. The pair had been responsible for some of the most expensive Disney products of the Eighties. Dealing with Carl Barks, a former Disney storyman and comic book artist (credited with creating the Uncle Scrooge character and dozens of others), Hamilton and Cochran produced numerous top selling items. Most prestigious was a series of limited edition lithographs (prints) of new paintings by Barks featuring Disney characters. Initially selling for under five hundred dollars, in a matter of years, the prints were selling for over ten thousand.

The pair came in, took stock of the art program and made various recommendations. Key was placing the art to new

productions in auction and letting the public set the price for the artwork. Sotheby's auction in 1989 of cels from *Who Framed Roger Rabbit* demonstrated that collectors were willing to pay top dollar for recent animation art. The same buying frenzy was seen in 1990 when cels from *The Little Mermaid* were sold in a similar auction. New cels were now valued from five hundred dollars and up. Prices on older artwork were naturally affected.

Throughout the Eighties, other studios like Warners, HannaBarbera, and Don Bluth began to release their animation art through dealers and it met with such unexpected success that today it is a normal practice. Unfortunately, not all the

Below:
Hand colored
model sheet
drawing.
© 1983 Tom
Carter
Productions

**Donald Duck
50th Birthday
Commemorative
Cel Portfolio**

studios had much to release. Cels from most of the classic cartoons no longer existed in any quantity.

When Warner Brothers needed more storage room in the '60s, the first thing to go was the animation art from the classic cartoons. According to one animator, there was so much artwork that they couldn't burn it all so they paid someone to drive out into the desert somewhere and bury it in an unmarked grave. Whether the story is accurate or not, the artwork did disappear and Warner Brothers, at the time, felt it was worthless. MGM did the same with their artwork in the early

Above: Promotional folder for a limited edition series of cels. ©1991 Walt Disney Company

Seventies.

To cash in on the fervor of the new animation collector, studios began producing limited edition cels. These cels were similar to limited edition fine art prints of classic and modern painters. Most were numbered and signed.

The most prolific producers of limited edition cels are the Walt Disney Company (scenes from their features and shorts) and Chuck Jones (Warner Brothers characters). Other studios offering limited edition cels include Warner Brothers, Hanna-Barbera and Don Bluth. Directors jumping on this bandwagon include Friz Freleng (Warner Brothers and Pink Panther), Robert McKimson (Warner Brothers), Bob Clampett (Warner Brothers and Beany & Cecil), and Shamus Culhane (Betty Boop).

Limited edition cels come in two styles: the creation from an existing piece of animation artwork (as is the case of the Disney Studios) or the creation of a cel based on a new piece of artwork (such as the Chuck Jones series). Generally, the cels produced from existing art are re-created with the same techniques of the original production cels with either hand inked or Xeroxed line and painted on the back. Less common are Serigraphs, which are created similar to silk screen. (The cel in the *Mickey Is Sixty* magazine,

from 1989, was a Serigraph.)

Whether or not such limited editions will rise in value as much as production cels is still uncertain. Many of the earliest Chuck Jones limited cels, from the Seventies are sold out. Some of these early ones have shown a dramatic increase in price. Limited edition cels offer attractive images suitable for framing (since they are all drawn or selected specifically for display), famous characters, and guaranteed authenticity. All at a price often less than an actual cel.

Perhaps the first question a buyer should ask is the reason for the purchase. Animation fans love cels because they are colorful and because they are an actual piece of the film. They are a physical souvenir of an emotional memory. They can also be viewed as another collectible art form in which the desire is only to purchase pieces that will rise in value. Luckily, both buyers should share several thoughts (and questions) in common when looking for a cel.

Image

Does the cel look good? Generally most collectors look for a large, complete image centered on the cel with the character's eyes open and an interesting expression. Finding such a cel is not always easy. The average cel was not photographed to appear in the family album or a high school yearbook. It was just one of many images of the character in motion.

The character's eyes might be going through a sequence of blinking with the eyelids at an odd position. The body may be in an awkward position, even turned away from the camera. A body part might be missing because that element was to be animated separately or because other objects were supposed to be in front of the character obscuring part of its body. The figure could be very small, because the figure needed to appear as being at a great distance away in the film. These flaws all lessen the value of the cel.

Origin

Where did the cel come from? This doesn't mean, "who was the previous owner?" Characters changed through the years and were often animated by different studios and for different purposes. A cel of Mighty Mouse might be a rare find from Terrytoons of the Forties, an animated commercial from the Fifties, Filmation's TV version of the Seventies, or even an Eighties interpretation from the studio of Ralph Bakshi.

You can not solely judge a cel's age or origin merely from the appearance of a character on it. A Disney character like Jiminy Cricket, Mickey Mouse or Donald Duck would have appeared in many places besides an

original short or feature of the Thirties and Forties. Along with the obvious recreations mentioned above, there are also educational films and publicity art.

Condition

What is the condition of the cel? Has it been repaired? Obviously one should check

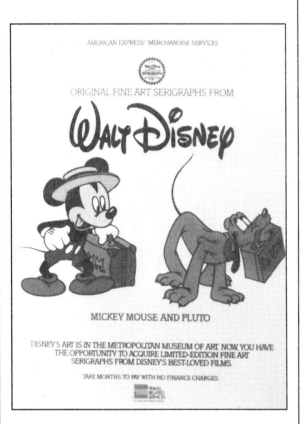

AMERICAN EXPRESS® MERCHANDISE SERVICES

ORIGINAL FINE ART SERIGRAPHS FROM

Walt Disney

MICKEY MOUSE AND PLUTO

DISNEY'S ART IS IN THE METROPOLITAN MUSEUM OF ART. NOW YOU HAVE THE OPPORTUNITY TO ACQUIRE LIMITED-EDITION FINE ART SERIGRAPHS FROM DISNEY'S BEST-LOVED FILMS.

TAKE MONTHS TO PAY WITH NO FINANCE CHARGES.

the physical condition of the cel. Since the beginning, there has not been a standard cel paint. Because the cel was considered merely a temporary step in the process of making the cartoon, the paint only had to remain on the cel long enough to be photographed.

Some early studios used cheap store-bought glue to mix in with the paint. It dried out quickly and in some cases discolored the artwork with age.

The paints of many classic cels can dehydrate and result in chipping and brittleness. Even the fragile cel itself was easily dented or torn, yellowed with age, scratched, damaged by tape or trimmed for a picture frame. These are only some of the reasons so few cels survived from the Golden Age of animation and why prices will continue to rise on the rarer pieces.

This also means that any cel can be in danger of being destroyed while in your collection. There are stories too numerous to print about buyers who bought a perfect cel only to have a "tiny crack" develop in the paint after the purchase (sometimes as shortly as one day). Some have seen their expensive art turn to dust before their eyes.

Newer cels are mostly painted with an acrylic paint. This paint is much more permanent and flexible. (So flexible that one can actually roll up a cel painted with acrylic paint. But that is not recommended.) One of the last studios to switch to acrylic based paint was the Disney studio, which didn't do so until the Eighties!

Within the last few years, several cel restoration companies have been created

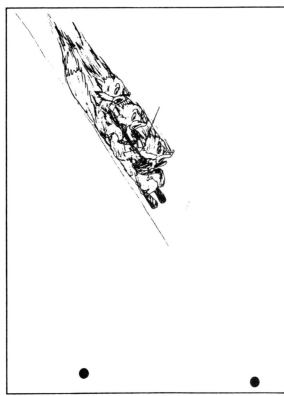

to repair, repaint and restore damaged cels. In most cases, this repair consists of scraping all the paint off of the cel and repainting the entire image. Some have claimed that this is nothing more than a "new painting on an old cel." At this time, re-stored cels should be clearly identified as such and in general are priced lower than unrestored cels.

Authenticity

Is it really a cel? It may look like a cel, and feel like a cel, but was it used in animation? Due to the growing number of books out which feature reproductions of animation art, it is becoming more easy to create forgeries. In the Seventies, an employee at Disneyland painted cels for fun. He used photocopies of original animation drawings from the studio. Some of the cels began showing up on cel dealer's lists. The '80s found a ring in Dallas that was painting cels of the Peanuts characters and selling them as animation art.

Many fanciful stories have been concocted to explain why the colors on a character look wrong. ("It's a night scene.") Other things to note might be Xerox lines on cels from films before 1960.

Seller

What is the background of your dealer? One of the best ways to assure authenticity is to know your seller. In the Seventies, many animation art dealers were merely collectibles or comic dealers selling cels. They weren't always certain what cels had come from what films.

Today there are many established galleries, mail order dealers and shops. Of course if you purchase from a larger gallery, the price will obviously be higher. They must cover their various expenses and overhead. Smaller dealers can often offer better prices, but may lack selection.

A good place to check for animation dealers would be in some of the magazines related to animation. *Animation Magazine* (VSD Publications, 6750 Centinela Avenue #300, Culver City, California 90230), *Animato* (PO Box 1240, Cambridge, Massachusetts 02238) and *StoryboarD/The Art of Laughter* (Laughter Publications, 80 Main Street, Nashua, New Hampshire 03060) feature many ads from animation art dealers.

Price

What is it really worth? Perhaps the toughest question. There are obvious guidelines that could apply. Older is more valuable than younger. A famous character is worth more than a secondary character. Big studios are better known than small studios. A good looking image will cost more than a poor one. However all of these guidelines, like all such rules of thumb, will have many exceptions.

One good way to get an idea is gather as many lists from dealers as possible. This will give the buyer an idea of how the prices range around the country. If lucky enough to live in an area where there are animation art galleries, visit them to see what prices range.

One key to remember is that all cels, like all original art, are one-of-a-kind items. (Excluding limited edition.) Two cels, from the very same film, with the very same character, from the very same scene could have two very different prices.

The final factor is your intention for the cel. If you are buying for pleasure, never pay more in price than the pleasure you will receive from it. The chance to have a favorite character, from a cherished film on the wall can be quite a valuable pleasure. Should investment be mainly on your mind, then check with as many experts as possible.

Getting Help

Luckily for newer collectors there is a large amount of information available. There are several good books available about the history of animation and animated characters. These will help the buyer find out more about the films and characters available. It will also help in spotting the era a cel may have come from and its general rarity.

Of more interest may be the magazines and societies aimed at the animation art buyer. In *Toon Magazine* (4640 Denny Avenue, Toluca Lake, California 91602) offers

articles and ads aimed at those buying art. The Animation Art Guild (330 West 45th Street, #9D, New York, New York 10036) offers a quarterly newsletter filled with articles relating to purchasing animation art (like upcoming auctions, recent prices, etc.). Even galleries are getting into publications. Cartoon Corner (2-C Gill Street, Wobrun, Massachusetts 01801) is a chain of galleries and offers "The Cel." Magic Moments (80 Main Street, Nashua, New Hampshire 03060) has "Feel the Magic" and their own limited edition cel of Arty the Animator, a canine cartoonist and spokesperson for the Art for Everyone Association!

An alternative to today's cel prices is to buy other forms of animated art. Animation drawings, storyboard sketches, inspirational sketches, and model sheets all offer many of the cel's best features. Though seldom in color, these items have the added desire of being the true art created for the film. These pieces are drawn by the artist. The cel, for all of its color, is still a traced and colored copy of the original artwork. Another nice thing about these alternatives is the price. A good pencil drawing may cost much less than the price of a cel of that same drawing although even pencil drawings are now starting to show a price

Opposite page: Two animation drawings from the '40s showing different studios' hole punching procedures. © MGM and Columbia

increase.

Cel Blocked

Despite the current increase in animation, fewer cels from modern productions are available. Most of the TV production for the past two decades has been done overseas. The cels are usually not shipped back to the United States. The expense for such a shipment would be prohibitive as well as the expense to store a studio's collection of cels. Only a few of these (some of Disney's TV series, the *Teenage Mutant Ninja Turtles*, *Alvin And The Chipmunks*, etc.) have been brought to the States to sell.

In 1988, Filmation closed. It was one of the last studios doing major TV production totally in the United States. They created animation in the past for shows starring the *Star Trek* crew, Archie and his friends, Bill Cosby, Jerry Lewis, Lassie, the Lone Ranger, Superman and more. After being sold to a foreign company, they nearly destroyed the entire cel library until an investor raised the money to buy the warehouse of over six million cels.

Also, in an attempt to cut costs, studios have experimented to have computers color the animation art rather than the laborious and expensive method of hand painting each cel. The success of those experiments can be seen in many places such as TV

(Hanna-Barbera's *The Smurfs*) and Disney's animated feature, *The Rescuers Down Under*. No production cels exist for animation produced this way. The coloring was done by computer in the computer. Since Disney has the original art, it would not stop them from using it to

Below:
Comic book art featuring animated characters, such as this cover of a Rocky and Bullwinkle comic, are also collected.
© Jay Ward

create cels for sale in the time honored fashion but they would not be production cels.

As the popularity and prices of animation art continue to grow, there are plans in the coming decade to expand the sale of animation art into gift shops and hobby outlets besides

the more formal galleries. When animation auctions began a few years ago, perhaps twenty people or so would attend a Christie's function. The auction held in June 1990 at Christies had several hundred crowded into the auction room.

For centuries alchemists around the world tried to turn simple base elements to gold. What they could not accomplish, animators did. They turned simple pencil graphite into a highly prized, highly priced collectible.

TOP SECRET

CHAPTER TWELVE:

SILENT NIGHT, ANIMATED BRIGHT: ANIMATED CHRISTMAS SPECIALS

Silent Night, Animated Bright: Animated Christmas Specials

What would Christmas be without the annual deluge of animated specials filling network, independent and cable channels? It would be 1961! Throughout animation's history almost every studio had at least one cartoon with a holiday theme but it never occurred to TV producers to develop animated Christmas specials until the early Sixties.

Though animation had proved successful on TV via repeats, new syndicated series and prime time series, it didn't enter the arena of holiday specials until 1962 with *Mr. Magoo's Christmas Carol*. After Magoo's success it still took almost a decade for animated holiday specials to finally take hold and become a permanent part of viewers' lives.

Christmas is for children of all ages. Many make that same claim of animation. The simple fact that most people can't remember a Christmas without animated Christmas specials illustrates how natural it was to mate the season to the medium.

Animation, like Christmas, seems to have a timelessness about it. An aura of fantasy and fanciful legends surround the Christmas season and animation has proven itself uniquely suited to handle the special demands of fantasy. Often times, the Christmas magic of flying reindeer, talking snowmen, and spirits of another time seem to be captured best by the Art of the animator.

As stated, many classic theatrical cartoons feature a Christmas theme and are as popular today as when they first appeared. It's not surprising to see such classics as Walt Disney's Silly Symphonies, *Santa's Workshop* (1932) and its sequel *The Night Before Christmas* (1933) popping up. Both of these early gems feature views of Santa's special job from his elves building toys to his fleet of magic reindeer.

Other shorts merely celebrate the time of year. *Pluto's Christmas Tree* (1952) has Pluto trying unsuccessfully to warn Mickey Mouse about Chip 'n' Dale hiding in the Christmas tree. *Bedtime For Sniffles* (1940), a Warner Brothers' cartoon directed by Chuck Jones, shows Sniffles the Mouse trying to stay awake for Santa Claus. The classic *Peace On Earth* (1939), an anti-war cartoon from MGM, uses the Christmas season as the framework for the story of the destruction of mankind. These and other Christmas cartoons have a special magic all their own.

The Small One, directed by Don Bluth while he was still at Disney, actually deals with the religious significance of the season. It tells of how John and Mary's trip to Bethlehem was made easier with the help of an aging donkey (the Small One) and his young owner. A large number of religious videocassette series, such as Hanna-Barbera's Greatest Stories Ever Told: Tales from the Bible, offer their versions on the origin of the holiday.

There are also a number of feature films that have the Winter holidays as key elements. Disney's *Lady And The Tramp* begins with Lady, as a puppy, being a Christmas gift and ends at another Christmas. The film also includes a lovely new variation of "Silent Night" by Peggy Lee. *101 Dalmatians,* another Disney classic, has Pongo, Perdita and 99 puppies return home just in time for the holidays. *An American Tail*, from Steven Spielberg and Don Bluth, opens with Fievel Mousekewitz and his family celebrating Hanukkah.

Though Christmas cartoons were not uncommon, the ever rerunning Christmas special was created less than three decades ago. For many years, the only animated treat during the Christmas season was *From All Of Us To All Of You.* Basically, the show was a series of holiday vignettes where Jiminy Cricket reveals Christmas cards that segue into scenes from Disney's animated features or shorts. Originally screened in 1958 as part of the *Disneyland* Television show, it was revived (and revised) year after year. For awhile, the only change each year was in the final segment, usually a clip to promote the Disney animated feature then showing in theaters. For years, the credits listed Jack Hannah as director. Hannah, well respected for his work as director on the Donald Duck theatrical shorts, was responsible for that first show but has philosophically remarked that "each year the material has gradually changed to freshen the show so that little of my work remains in the show now."

It wasn't until 1962 that the first made for television animated Christmas special premiered. Since that time, nearly 100 animated Christmas specials have glutted the airwaves; some appearing as early as November on the networks. The eventual success of the Christmas animated show spawned an ever expanding flood of animation that has already engulfed other holidays from Halloween to Mother's Day to Arbor Day. Few holidays remain untouched by the deluge.

This flood began with the first, and still one of the best, animated Christmas programs made especially for television: *Mr. Magoo's Christmas Carol* (now available on both videotape and Laserdisc). In 1962, the myopic Magoo had fallen on bad times. U.P.A., the studio that produced Magoo shorts, had cut back on production of short cartoons, and the

company had been sold so that the original creators were no longer involved. Under the direction of President Henry Saperstein, U.P.A. was seeking to enter the television market and regenerate lost income from the theatrical market. An earlier foray into television, *The Gerald McBoing Boing Show,* had met with limited success.

Quincy Magoo, still visible in the public eye as the pitchman for General Electric ("It's easy to see, the best bulbs are GE," as Magoo would state in TV commercials), was U.P.A.'s strongest asset. Directed by Abe Levitow from an adaptation by Barbara Chain of Dickens' classic story, *Mr. Magoo's Christmas Carol* casts the irascible Magoo in the role of Ebenezer Scrooge. The special was commissioned by the Timex watch company.

It is an hour long original musical retelling of the miser visited by three spirits of Christmas. The story is told as if Magoo were playing the role in a stage production. The show opens with Magoo, in typical style creating havoc with his nearsightedness as he heads to the theater and gets into his costume. Once the curtain goes up, he plays the Scrooge character straight. Only an occasional mention of his lack of sight is made, and this is usually explained away as part of Scrooge 's

Above: Cover of children's book version of the classic special. © UPA

stinginess in not buying glasses nor spending more for better lighting. The special is a fairly straight forward adaptation of the original classic tale.

Strong voice work by such professionals as Jim Backus (as the voice of Magoo), Morey Amsterdam, Jack Cassidy, Paul Frees and Les Tremayne among others brought the special a rich personality. The story was highlighted by Jule Styne 's and Bob Merrill's memorable songs including "A Hand For Each Hand," "Ringle Ringle," and "It's Great To Be Back On Broadway."

The special was such a success that it was repeated the following year and rated so highly that NBC decided to develop a half hour prime time series with Magoo playing classic characters like Cyrano, Captain Ahab and D'Artagnan. *The Famous Adventures Of Mr. Magoo* lasted one season pitted against the first year of *Gilligan's Island* while *Mr. Magoo's Christmas Carol*

Below:
Young Rudolph and family.
© Rankin Bass

continues to delight audiences each holiday season.

Amazingly, high level executives still hadn't realized that it wasn't just the fascination of Magoo playing a classic character that enthralled audiences; it was the combination of

Christmas and animation. It took three more major Christmas successes before that realization occurred and the flood of specials began.

In 1964, Rankin-Bass released a puppet animated (called "Animagic") special, *Rudolph The Red-Nosed Reindeer* (available on

videotape and Laserdisc), based on the long-popular song by Johnny Marks. Romeo Muller, who would become one of the most prolific writers of animated specials, enhanced the song's story of Rudolph's difficulties growing up as a "freak."

The story is told as a flashback as a folksy snowman named Sam recounts the year there almost wasn't a Christmas because of bad weather. Rudolph is seen as a young deer with a "defect." His parents try to hide it, but it is soon discovered and the reindeer all agree "not to let Rudolph play in any Reindeer games." The only one not bothered by his nose is a female doe, Clarice. This story is somewhat parralled by an Elf named Herbie. Herbie doesn't like making toys, he wants to be a dentist. This is a shock to his boss who knows all elves love to make toys.

Both outcasts meet and decide to run off. On the journey, the pair meet a wacky prospector, visit the Island of Misfit Toys, and battle the Abominable snowman. When all return to Santa's headquarters, Santa tries to announce that Christmas is being canceled due to the bad storm, but keeps getting blinded by Rudolph 's shining nose. It suddenly comes to Santa that Rudolph 's nose will be the light necessary to fly.

Christmas is saved, Herbie gets to be a dentist and Santa finds homes for all the Misfit Toys.

Original composer Marks wrote seven new songs for the special that include such tunes as "Silver and Gold" and "Holly Jolly Christmas." Several of the songs were sung by the snowman narrator, Burl Ives. *Rudolph* was a huge success in the ratings, earning it a spot in the growing annual TV lineup of animated holiday specials. In 1986 it achieved the distinction of being the longest consecutively aired animated special. Its success inspired two similar sequels, *Rudolph's Shiny New Year* (1976) with Red Skelton as Father Time/Narrator and *Rudolph And Frosty* (1979) with Mickey Rooney as Santa Claus. Billy Richards provided Rudolph's voice in all three specials.

After *Mr. Magoo's Christmas Carol* and *Rudolph The Red-Nosed Reindeer*, networks and sponsors saw the possibility of profiting with animated Christmas specials. For two years, Lee Mendelson had tried to sell a documentary he had completed on Peanuts' cartoonist Charles Schulz. He previewed the show for Coca-Cola but they weren't interested in sponsoring it either. However, they asked Mendelson if Schulz had a Christmas special they might purchase. Mendelson assured them he did, went

© 1981 United Feature Syndicate

*Above:
Artwork
promoting the first
Peanuts' special.
© United
Features
Syndicate*

home and called Schulz and told him to write a quick outline of a Christmas special because Coca-Cola representatives needed it by Monday. Mendelson was making this call on Friday night.

The outline had to be sent by telegram because there was no time to mail it (and this was pre-"fax" days). "They bought it off a telegram," recalled Mendelson, "Originally Sparky (Schulz) said there was to be no laugh track. But in 1965 everything had laugh tracks and I said we had to have a laugh track. Schulz said, 'Then we don't do the show.' So we didn't have a laugh track.

"You only get one shot in this business. If we'd blown that first show, Peanuts would not have come to television. When we finished

Silent Night, Animated Bright: Animated Christmas Specials

Above:
The Grinch and Max.
© MGM

the production, Bill (animator Bill Melendez) and I thought we'd failed. The head man at the network said the show was just awful. I kind of agreed with him but Schulz and the sponsor loved the show."

The public agreed with Schulz and the sponsor. The production cost for *A Charlie Brown Christmas* (available on videotape) in 1965 was reported at approximately $100,000 and its success spawned countless other Peanuts specials. It won a Peabody Award for Outstanding Children's Program and an Emmy for Outstanding Children's Program, the first time an animated special won the honor. (Previous winners were TV series.)

Schulz wrote the final script and it was directed by Bill Melendez who had previously done some animated commercials featuring the Peanuts' characters. The story recounts the misadventures of Charlie Brown as he becomes progressively more upset by the holiday commercialism of his friends. The rehearsal of a Christmas pageant allows Linus the opportunity to remind everyone of the true meaning of Christmas.

At the time, there was great debate about whether they should use children's voices for the characters or if they should have adults portraying kids. History has shown that the right decision was made to use children's voices.

Wanting to get away from the sound of the usual "cartoon music," they asked a San Francisco composer-musician to develop a jazz oriented score for the special. The music was so well received that Vince Guaraldi and his trio went on to compose and perform all of the music for the first sixteen Peanuts TV specials until his untimely death. "His musical genius deserves a great deal of the credit for the success of the television specials," stated Schulz.

The success of these specials inspired producers to seek out other properties that might be adapted to animated Christmas specials. Chuck Jones, then head of MGM animation, remembered during World War II collaborating with Theodor "Dr. Seuss" Geisel on training films starring a character named "Private SNAFU." Jones approached Seuss with the idea of animating Seuss' book, *How The Grinch Stole Christmas.* Ten months later, it lit up the Christmas season (now available on videotape and

Laserdisc). As (then) syndicated entertainment writer Marian Dern described it at the time, "it succeeds because it was not made *For* kids, or *For* the season, but *From* the creative talents and imagination and sense of fun of the two of them, and the staff who worked on it."

Dr. Seuss is credited with the script and lyrics while Albert Hague, now known for his role as a teacher on the TV series *Fame*, did the music. Songs like "You're A Mean One, Mr. Grinch," sung in the special by Thurl Ravenscroft (the voice of Tony the Tiger), still sparkle after two decades. Chuck Jones was the producer-director and it was generally regarded as Jones' finest work since leaving Bugs Bunny and friends at Warner Brothers.

The special, narrated by Boris Karloff, tells the story of the Grinch who hates Christmas because of the Whos of Whoville Christmas celebration noise. He devises a plan to steal Christmas by disguising himself as Santa (and his dog as a reindeer) and stealing every gift, decoration and tree. The Grinch is forced to rethink his ideas when, to his surprise, the Whos celebrate Christmas "without boxes, ribbons and tags." The special won the Peabody Award for television programming excellence.

"Investing in quality programs ultimately pays much more," commented Jones in the late Seventies during one of the yearly revivals of his special. "*The Grinch* cost about $350,000 to make and has earned many times that amount over the years." At the time, it was the highest price ever paid for a cartoon special.

By the late Sixties, almost every animation studio was preparing a television Christmas special. Where *Mr. Magoo's Christmas Carol*'s budget could be measured in thousands of dollars, Rankin-Bass's version, *The Stingiest Man In Town* (1968), featuring a caricature of Walter Matthau as Scrooge, cost over a million and a half dollars. In fact, Rankin-Bass became a chief supplier of the genre, producing almost a dozen Christmas specials featuring traditional animation and stop-motion puppet animation. *Frosty The Snowman* (1969), *'Twas The Night Before Christmas* (1974), *Frosty's Winter Wonderland* (1976) and others all had a consistency thanks to the character designs of Paul Coker, Jr., perhaps best known for his work in *MAD* magazine.

Most new Christmas specials seemed to look to the first four for inspiration. Magoo's success led others to revive or showcase popular animated characters. Bugs Bunny was featured in *Bugs Bunny's Looney Christmas Tales* (1980), a

Below: Paul Coker Jr. ad art promoting Rankin Bass Christmas specials. © Rankin Bass

series of three new shorts: a parody of Dickens' *Christmas Carol* with Yosemite Sam as Scrooge and Tweety Pie as Tiny Tim; the Coyote and Road Runner in a snow chase; and Bugs Bunny and his nephew Clyde battle the Tasmanian Devil in a Santa suit. Casper the Friendly Ghost was in *Casper's First Christmas* (1979). *The Pink Panther In A Pink Christmas* (1978) starred the silent panther trying to find a home during the holiday, a story based loosely on O'Henry's "The Cop and the

Below:
The Pink Panther's Christmas special was adapted for his comic book series.
©1978 UAC-Geoffrey

Anthem." Disney went all the way back to the beginning by doing its own version of Dickens' tale, *Mickey's Christmas Carol* (1983). This theatrical featurette had Uncle Scrooge (now best known for *Duck Tales*) as Scrooge and Mickey in the minor role of Bob Crachit, the mouse's first theatrical outing in 30 years. It substituted other Disney characters for the other characters in the story.

TV characters seemed especially appropriate for converting to holiday specials. Yogi Bear appeared in *Yogi Bear's Christmas Caper* (1982), a half hour special and *Yogi's First Christmas* (1980) a made for TV movie advertised as "more colorful than *Fantasia*." The Flintstones starred in *A Flintstone Christmas* (1977), the first time Fred and Barney had appeared in a prime time show since 1966. The Smurfs appeared in two Christmas specials: *The Smurfs' Christmas Special* (1982) and *'Tis The Season To Be Smurfy* (1987). 'Other producers looked to *A Charlie Brown Christmas* and brought comic strip characters into the holidays. *B.C.: A Special Christmas* (1971) featured two of the cave folk found in Johnny Hart's comic strip about prehistoric people trying to invent a holiday in order to sell merchandise. *Ziggy's Gift* (1982) had Ziggy assisting those less fortunate than

himself as a street corner Santa. *Garfield's Christmas* (1987) had Jim Davis' fat cat spend the holidays with Jon's family on the farm.

Some looked at *Grinch* and began looking for books and stories to adapt. Frank L. Baum, who created the world of Oz, also wrote the book used for *The Life And Adventures Of Santa Claus* (1985). *The Stingiest Man In Town* (1978) was another adaptation of Dickens' Christmas Carol, this time with a Walter Matthau voicing Scrooge. (The special was based on a version produced for live action TV in the Fifties.) The last Babar book written by the original author, Jean de Brunhoff, became *Babar And Father Christmas* (1986)

While some studios followed *Rudolph*'s lead and just looked for any well known characters. Frosty the Snowman starred in several specials for Rankin-Bass. *A Very Merry Cricket* (1973), from Chuck Jones, used characters from his popular special *The Cricket In Times Square* (1972). Even the Little Rascals were revived in animated form for *The Little Rascals Christmas Special* (1979).

Some of the best Christmas specials were the work of independents. In 1971, Richard Williams, currently enjoying popularity from his work on *Who Framed Roger Rabbit*, animated a version of

Dickens' Christmas Carol basing the look on illustrations from 19th century London. It was the only television film ever nominated for an Academy Award because it had received some theatrical distribution prior to appearing on TV, as well as later. More amazingly, it won the Oscar.

Nelvana, a Canadian studio responsible for such hit animated series as *Beetlejuice* and features as *The Care Bears Movie* began its career with *A Cosmic Christmas* (1977). It told about three aliens who come to Earth in search of the meaning of the Star of Bethlehem. Even PBS had its own animated Christmas special, *Simple Gifts: Six Episodes For Christmas* (1978). And Wil Vinton won an Emmy for his *Claymation Christmas Starring The California Raisins* (1987).

The mating of Christmas and animation hasn't been totally free from disappointments. Some producers feel they can use the good will of the season to compensate for small budgets and even smaller inspiration. They insist on devising holiday specials that lack coherent stories or feature poorly developed characters or rely on animation that moves so slightly or so jerkily that it hardly deserves to be called animation. Many of the Christmas specials during

the last decade also seem to be caught in a conflict that has spilled over from the Saturday morning battleground; should animated shows merely entertain or should they also educate?

Dr. Gordon Berry, co-ordinator of a panel of educators and psychologists who acted as story consultants for the *Fat Albert* programs including the Christmas special, stated, "The stories are designed to entertain youngsters while guiding them in the development of judgment and moral values. Since adults are post graduate

Above: Yogi and company celebrate Yogi's First Christmas. © *Hanna-Barbera*

children, they can benefit from the same guidance." Dr. Berry spoke very highly of the educational values in the *Fat Albert Christmas Special* (1977) where children learn that adults can have problems as well. The story had the gang try to help out an expectant mother and her down-and-out family who have taken refuge in their clubhouse.

At an industry screening of the *Fat Albert* programs, more than half the audience walked out, prompting Joe Barbera of Hanna-Barbera to remark that he yearned for a return to the old days so that "when a cat chases a mouse,

Silent Night, Animated Bright: Animated Christmas Specials

he doesn't have to stop and teach him how to blow glass or weave a basket. My wish for Christmas is that they would leave education to the schools and entertainment to us."

The debate between purely entertainment oriented specials or educational animated specials is still fully unresolved. More recently another related debate has risen, that being since they are closely tied to such a religious holiday, how reverent should they be? Some more recent specials created a stir in that area.

A Garfield Christmas (1987) worried some executives at CBS who felt that the special "didn't do anything." However, that was creator's Jim Davis' point. He stated that he "didn't want to do another special where someone learns the meaning of Christmas or has to 'save' the holiday." Davis wanted to create a "typical" Christmas in where a family gets together, has a little fun, eats a lot of food and exchanges gifts. "There's magic to such simplicity," thought Davis. Whether CBS's fears were justified or not, the special went on to be the highest rated animated special of the year.

It's CBS companion, the Emmy-winning *A Claymation Christmas* came under the fire of a number of religious groups. They felt the special,

Below: Animation drawing from an unproduced Daffy Duck Christmas short. © Warner Brothers

a series of Christmas carols turned Claymation music videos, were detrimental to the "true" spirit of Christmas. The most criticized number being a jazzed-up version of "We Three Kings" sung by hip camels.

As the Nineties begin, the production of animated Christmas specials shows only slight signs of abating. In 1989, even the Simpsons preceded their successful Fox TV series with a half hour Christmas special where Homer tries to earn extra money by working as a Santa Claus. However, more and more, the debuting specials appear on cable,

syndication or home video rather than network TV.

No doubt, as each new holiday season arrives, new cartoons will join with traditional favorites and the flickering colored images will dance like visions of sugar plums. Some of these new productions will join the ever growing population of forgotten specials and some will become classics and live healthy lives via TV repeats and home video. But all will owe a debt to those first animated Christmas specials which continue to have the holiday spirit and still sparkle as brightly as the more expensive new shows.

TOP SECRET
CHAPTER THIRTEEN:

BORN AGAIN
TOONS

Born Again Toons

Death is not always a permanent situation in the world of animation. Besides the obvious ease that such characters as Wile E. Coyote, Tom (Cat), Peg Leg Pete, Brain (Inspector Gadget's dog) and others sustain deadly falls, knives and explosions, some characters have even been able to rise from the grave, or ashes of past animated lives.

These Phoenix-like characters don't always have a successful second life, or third, or fourth, or fifth (or more), but few toons aren't

Below:
Felix, the TV version, with his magic bag of tricks.
© Pat Sullivan/ King Features

willing to give a second career a chance. For every animated star who makes a successful comeback, there are more who find the second time around isn't necessarily better.

Reincarnated characters never know how they will return to the screen. Stars of features or theatrical shorts might be given new life on Saturday morning. Sometimes the later lives of these characters are quite different than their original life. In fact, there are times the revival is better received

or better remembered than the original.

Felix the Cat is an excellent example of life being better (remembered) the second time around. The most popular animated character of silent cinema, Felix, was created by Otto Messmer for a one shot cartoon that eventually led into a series of over 100 silent adventures for this fantastic feline.

In his silent cartoons Felix was a rough and tumble Tomcat who never passed up an opportunity for

a little mischief, even if it was malicious. Independent, resourceful and a little mystical, he would shift between being someone's house pet to being a vagabond wanderer to a down-on-his-luck little Charlie Chaplin. Audiences loved the silent Felix whose independence and cocky self-confidence were key qualities that made him a star. Although he never talked, his pantomimic skill made him an international celebrity.

He reappeared in 1936 as a talking character in three color cartoons. His character was altered so that he was a happy, helpful character with a little boy's voice. He was no longer the instigator of action but merely an observer. Under the direction of Disney's Burt Gillett, Felix tried to copy unsuccessfully the "cute" Mickey Mouse. These three cartoons from Van Beuren didn't truly kill Felix; he continued on for decades in comic books and a newspaper strip done by his creator, Otto Messmer.

However, his third film life came in the late Fifties when Joe Oriolo (creator of Casper the Friendly Ghost) acquired the rights to Felix and produced a series of cartoons for TV. Oriolo had been an assistant to Messmer. It is this Felix, with his "magic bag of tricks" that is the best remembered life of this feline thanks to

continuing merchandising efforts that use Oriolo's revised and simplified design of Felix and his bag. The ever changing bag substituted for the silent Felix's amazing ability to detach parts of his body and use them for a variety of purposes. Supplying Felix's voice (as well as the rest of the cast) was Jack Mercer, familiar to audiences as the voice of Popeye.

These shorts followed Felix in a string of cliff-hanging stories often featuring such villains as The Master Cylinder, The Professor and Rock Bottom. Of course there was also Felix's occasional friend, Poindexter, The Professor's nephew. Only 260 four-minute segments were done, and their continual availability in re-runs, and now on video, have kept this life alive. It was this Fifties' version that was the basis for *Felix The Cat: The Movie.* (Completed in 1989, the film has never received a U.S. theatrical release.) In his third life, Felix achieved as much fame as in his first life.

Another success story for second-time toons is that of Alvin and the Chipmunks. However the full success of this reincarnation is somewhat in debate. This argument is due to the fact that, unlike the first life of Felix which was almost unknown to those who discovered him in the Fifties, the Chipmunks' first

Above:
The original silent Felix, with his creator Otto Messmer.
© Pat Sullivan/ King Features

appearance is well remembered.

Alvin and his brothers began their animated career in 1961 with a prime time network half-hour program entitled *The Alvin Show.* About elementary school age, the chipmunks participated in typical domestic adventures with David Seville as their manager and guardian. One or two segments in each show were almost like animated music videos with the chipmunks singing their songs and popular favorites like "Home on the Range."

When the series left prime time, it appeared for a number of years on Saturday morning. However by the end of the Sixties, Bagdasarian had lost interest and so, apparently had the public and networks. In 1977, Bagdasarian's son, Ross, Jr. decided to revive the group. He found little interest in the mostly forgotten Superstars. NBC agreed to run the original series one season on Saturday morning in 1979 and it was well received.

What made the difference was a disc jockey who jokingly took a New Wave record, boosted the speed, and played it on the air as an example of "Chipmunk Punk." Radio shows and record shops were flooded with requests for the imaginary album. Ross Jr. contacted a small record distributor and released in June 1980 *Chipmunk Punk,* the first new Chipmunk album since 1967.

They were a hit and soon became an animated special and later a series on Saturday morning that lasted eight years! However, these newer chipmunks were quite different than the originals.

The angular, sparse, stylized design of the original series was dropped for a more round, cuter approach. The original series was more sharp, with Alvin almost an early day Bart Simpson. The newer chipmunks were softer and sweeter and more socially conscious in the personality department. The bite was removed so that they would

Opposite Page: Pebbles grows up for Pebbles And Bamm Bamm. © 1971 Hanna-Barbera

be more merchandisable and more in tune with the harsher restrictions on animated series in the early Eighties.

Those who remembered and loved the original trio often complained that the new group was nothing more than a bland shadow of the former characters. Children, who didn't know of the chipmunks' first life loved the new ones. The fact that the revived form survived almost three times as long as the original series, and even spawned a feature film, shows that the new format was successful, even if it lacked some of Ross Sr.'s original concept.

In many ways, it was the success of the Chipmunk revival, along with the move away from series based on merchandise concepts, that led to the largest period of animated reincarnation during the Eighties. Saturday morning network executives felt that audience awareness of a property was key to a new series' success. Such characters as Popeye, the Pink Panther, Mighty Mouse, Beany & Cecil and others found themselves dragged away from the comfortable world of old reruns and dressed up and converted to formats for Saturday morning.

Actually, such Saturday morning conversions were not new. Especially for series that began on TV. As seen in the Chipmunks, after they

left prime time, they were repeated for several seasons on Saturday morning. By the end of the '60s, the networks were removing most of the repeat shows (except for the continually popular Warner Brother shorts which appeared in variously titled shows). As replacements, some of these stars began moving into new lives on new Saturday morning shows.

Hanna-Barbera was quickest to re-use their popular characters. Yogi Bear found himself teamed with numerous other formerly syndicated characters like Huckleberry Hound, Pixie & Dixie, Snagglepuss, etc., and the Flintstones became fodder for the animation mixmaster.

The first to be converted was the Flintstones in 1971. *Pebbles And Bamm And Bamm* featured Fred, Wilma, Barney and Betty at about the same age as in the prime time series, but their children were now teen-agers. The adults were now merely supporting characters in a new teen oriented show, then popular on Saturday mornings. This series would be the first of many that tried to use the Flintstone name to sell a "new" show.

Fred and Barney soon found themselves teamed with everyone from Al Capp's Schmoo to Marvel Comics' The Thing (who had also become a teenager). Betty and Wilma served as

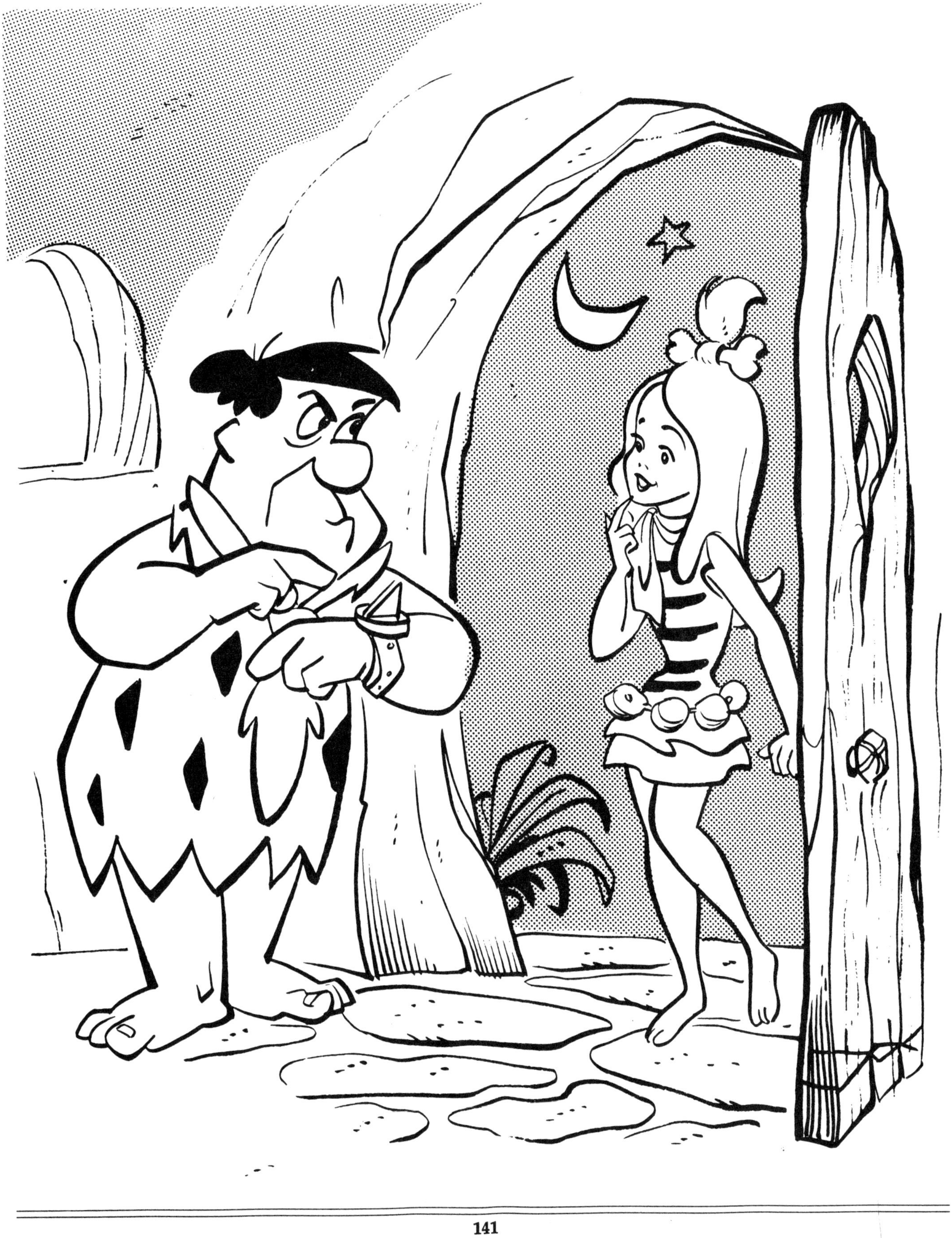

surrogate Lois Lanes to Captain Caveman.

Perhaps the one taking the most liberties was *The Flintstone Kids*. Debuting in 1986, the series was part of the de-evolving of characters made prominent with the Saturday morning hit, *The Muppet Babies*. This series actually re-wrote Flintstone history by having the characters appear as school friends. (According to the original series, Fred and Barney first meeting with Wilma and Betty was as adults at a social event.)

H-B's other most re-curring re-incarnation was Yogi Bear, beginning in 1972 with *Yogi's Ark Lark* an ABC *Saturday Superstar Movie* that gave birth to the Saturday morning series *Yogi's Gang*. Like most of Yogi's later incarnations, he was the leader of a group of H-B Superstars. For most of these newer lives, Yogi was fairly changed. No longer merely a non-conformist, mooching bear in Jellystone park, the new Yogi was generally a leader looked up to by other characters who would never steal picnic baskets. He could be a sportsman (*Laff-A-Lympics*), a spaceman (*Yogi's Galaxy Goof Ups*) or a race car driver (*Fender Bender 500*, part of *Wake Rattle And Roll*).

Yogi was reverted back to his old self in 1988 when Hanna Barbera produced a series of new shorts to help fill out a syndicated series that featured the old Yogi

shorts of the Fifties and early Sixties. These new shorts seldom had the life, pacing and style of the originals, but Yogi is at least (generally) back in Jellystone trying to have a good time.

Speaking of these later Yogi shorts, many times, series are simply "continued" years later. These new versions are more like different directions than lives. Such popular series as *The Jetsons*, *Space Ghost*, *Herculoids* and *Jonny Quest* had new episodes made years after the original series had concluded.

These newer episodes sometimes featured updated costumes or an additional character, but for the most part were attempts to revive a series rather than re-create it. Often this was done to make a more acceptable syndicated package. Sometimes new restrictions on violence, greater social awareness, and a drastic change in creative personnel resulted in the new product seeming humorless or without the magic and sparkle that made the original so memorable.

Then there are those stars who simply "re-appeared" with no real change. Mickey Mouse, and other Disney characters were newly animated for *Mickey's Christmas Carol*, the first of a slowly continuing series of Mickey featurettes. It was the first new theatrical Mickey animation in almost three

decades. Bugs Bunny appeared in a new theatrical short, Box Office Bunny (1990). Universal is allegedly working on doing a new Woody Woodpecker short for theaters.

Droopy, another former theatrical star has made a successful comeback thanks to the Roger Rabbit shorts from Disney. He even received his own series of TV segments as part of Fox's *Tom And Jerry Kids Show* where he appeared with a son. In fact, *Who Framed Roger Rabbit* brought many theatrical cartoon Superstars back to the big screen for some of their first new animation in decades. Once again, these were more like comebacks than revivals.

Though not all reincarnations have had the staying power of the new Chipmunks, some have had some notable success. Key among them was *Mighty Mouse: The New Adventures*. Bakshi's new version of the classic Terrytoon character not only changed a bit of the Mighty Mouse legend, it changed the look of TV animation. With the considerable help of various younger talents such as John Krisfaluci, Bob Jacques, and Kent Butterworth, Bakshi created a manic world of wild characters, strange takes and a sharp graphic look not usually seen on commercial TV.

This new series gave Mighty a new origin and

secret identity. Filmation had tried continuing the character in 1979 with *The New Adventures Of Mighty Mouse And Heckle And Jeckle* but were unable to duplicate the simple charm of the original Terrytoons. Bakshi's version kept the basic outline of the character but had little respect for the mouse's past history. The writing was at times sharp and clever. Other times it was self-indulgent and too impressed with itself. However it was never static, predictable or formula.

Critics came to the forefront calling it one of the best shows ever done for Saturday morning. Classic Warner Brothers director Chuck Jones said, "The Bakshi version of Mighty Mouse will help clear the air of the smog of spoiled sugar and superslop." Unfortunately, audiences weren't as impressed. Low ratings and a scandal over a scene in which a religious group claimed they saw Mighty Mouse sniff cocaine, killed the show after only two seasons.

Another show that proved somewhat successful, but not long lived was *A Pup Named Scooby Doo*. Using the same fountain of youth that gave viewers *Muppet Babies*, *The Flintstones Kids* and others, Hanna-Barbera re-created Scooby-Doo and the rest of his friends.

Scooby was already one of their most successful characters. Created in 1969, he was a last minute addition to a show about four teenagers solving mysteries. The show was highly successful and created numerous clones. After several years, though, the formula stalled and ratings began to sink. In 1985 a slightly new direction was tried with *The Thirteen Ghosts Of Scooby Doo*. Each week Scooby, Shaggy and Scrappy had to recapture one of thirteen ghosts who had escaped from a box. It met with more mediocre ratings and lasted only the one season.

Pup took much of the same direction as *Mighty Mouse The New Adventures*. Wild takes and wacky action took center stage. The series even poked fun at its previous versions with asides and jokes about how the old stories and villains were handled. The show was lively and received generally good critical reaction. Ratings were okay, but not enough to let it run past its second season of new episodes. (A third season of repeats only was run.) In many ways, the work on Bakshi's Mighty Mouse and Pup were the precursors to the wild antics found on *Tiny Toons*.

Some revivals had no success at all. DIC's recent attempt to bring *Beany And Cecil* back turned into one of Saturday morning's most embarrassing moments.

Canceled after five shows, it is one of the few animated series to be canceled in mid-production while airing. This new version of Bob Clampett's popular sea serpent and boy, still featured many of the original elements, including the cast of characters, use of puns and modern references and crazy sight gags.

However this new version was harsh, frantic and cold. Lost was the subtleness of character, the warmth of personality and general control found in Clampett's original. What could have been an ideal revival, or continuation, was thwarted by the desires of one group to create a more manic, more "modern" version battling another group who wanted the characters softer and nicer. It was a show that couldn't make up its mind as to what it wanted to be. As a result, it ended up being nothing but a hodge-podge of ideas and a curious footnote in animation history.

There are other revivals that almost everyone (viewers, characters, and those who worked on the shows) would probably prefer to forget. In 1978 Popeye was brought back in Hanna-Barbera's *The All New Popeye Hour* where within the limits of Saturday morning kidvid restrictions, they tried to recapture the spirit of the earlier Fleischer/ Famous Popeye cartoons.

Born Again Toons

1987 gave the world *Popeye And Son*. Popeye's son looked normal, not at all like his dad or mother (Olive Oyl), but had inherited his father's spinach powered strength. Popeye abandoned his familiar pipe and sailor suit and now wore Hawaiian shirts. Popeye, like Fred Flintstone before him, was now a supporting character to his teenaged child.

Another new father found in only a supporting role was The Pink Panther. He had to suffer through *Pink Panther And Sons* (1984).

Above: Animation drawing of Tom from a classic MGM short. © MGM

Right Top: Animation drawing from Filmation series © Filmation

Right Bottom: Model sheet poses for Hanna-Barbera's TV Version. © Hanna-Barbera Productions

Luckily he didn't appear much in the series, so wasn't too embarrassed. An attempt to put him in a prime time series as a talking character also failed.

Tom and Jerry were forced to become pals when Hanna-Barbera decided to make new shorts featuring the famous team they created. In *The Great Grape Ape/Tom And Jerry Show* (1975), this classic team simply stood around and watched other (talking) characters handle the comedy. Oddly, in the

proposed Tom and Jerry feature for 1992, the pair will again be shown as friends rather than friendly enemies.

From some of these born-again stories, one would feel that characters need be fairly old before being revamped. This is not true. *He-Man And The Masters Of The Universe* was a syndicated series key to creating the boom of new TV animation (and animation based on merchandise) in the mid-Eighties. It was a popular character and series for several years. Mattel produced the toys, Filmation the animation.

Based on several popular superhero legends, He-Man was the secret identity of Prince Adam of Eternia. Eternia was a world of sword, sorcery and science. His father was a native, but his mother was an astronaut from Earth. By raising a magic sword he and his pet tiger were transformed into the mighty hero and his fierce companion. Skeletor, an evil sorcerer, was continually trying to control the planet.

Both the series and toyline soon were replaced with new properties and shows. In a bid to regain some of the market Mattel

revamped the concept and in 1990 a new He-Man emerged. In this new version, He-Man was

sumoned to the future by the humans of planet Primus. Primus, a member of the Tri-Solar Galaxy, was at war with a skullface-shaped planet of mutants who were allied with Skeletor.

Nothing remained of the old scenes and even He-Man and Skeletor were redesigned to be less bulky and their personalities were altered slightly. When Adam, no longer Prince Adam, raised his sword to change, he shouted "By the power of Eternia" rather than "By the power of Grayskull." The new adventures were outer space oriented with space ship battles and a new supporting cast. The only remnants of

Born Again Toons

sorcery were He-Man's sword and Skeletor's power staff.

Just as the networks still try to develop popular movies into TV series, while the survival rate for such transitions is poor, studios and owners continue to update their characters. Sometimes it's merely a visual update, other times it's a complete overhaul. Though some of these new versions will no doubt catch the eye of new audiences

Below and at right: He-Man old and new. © Mattel

and become successful on their own, generally it will only cause original fans to grimace.

Characters become popular because of what they are. When they fall out of grace, they should be given some respect. Those who want to revive them should only do so by staying close to the original concept. The key word is "revive," not "revise." Characters forced to be re-born into some ghastly new version

might come to the same conclusion Frankenstein's monster did in the original *Bride Of Frankenstein*, when he told his ghastly bride, "We belong dead."

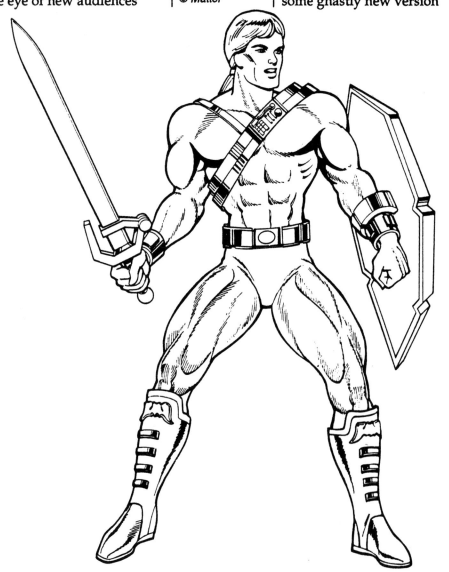

YOGI BEAR

By Hanna-Barbera

NO DOGS ALLOWED IN PARK EXCEPT ON LEASH.

12-17

McNaught Syndicate, Inc.

TOP SECRET

CHAPTER FOURTEEN:

ANIMATED STRIPPING

Before the days of reruns and VCRs, most animation fans had to wait for a cartoon to pop up at a movie theater, a nostalgia convention or on a local kiddie TV show if they wanted to see their favorite character. Before the Fifties, even some of those options did not exist. In order to cash in on the popularity of these characters, and keep them fresh in the minds of audiences, studios often licensed their top cartoon stars to appear in new adventures in comic books and comic strips.

The connection between animated cartoons and newspaper strips is even closer than the bond between books and movies. In a sense, newspaper strips not only inspired the creation of animation as it is known today, but provided the source for some of the first animated cartoon stars.

One of the real "fathers" of animation was Winsor McCay, a newspaper cartoonist best known for his popular *Little Nemo In Slumberland* which first appeared in 1905. Fascinated by the early experiments in animation, McCay produced and drew his first animated cartoon, *Little Nemo*. It was released in 1909, although some sources indicate that it did not receive wide distribution until 1911. The cartoon closely followed the strip and featured all the familiar characters including Little Nemo himself, the Princess, Flip, and Impy the cannibal. The cartoon's success prompted McCay to further explore animation, eventually creating Gertie the dinosaur, usually credited as being the first original animated star.

William Randolph Hearst founded International Film Service in 1916 for the express purpose of creating animated films based on the comic strips syndicated in the Hearst papers. *The Katzenjammer Kids* was the first project for the studio and these cartoons were quickly followed by others starring Happy Hooligan, Jiggs and Maggie, and Krazy Kat. The Krazy Kat cartoons of 1916 and 1917 were supervised by artist George Herriman, himself. They were one minute shorts appearing at the end of Hearst's weekly newsreels shown in movie theaters.

Also in 1916, Barre and Powers set up an animation studio to produce cartoons about the adventures of Mutt and Jeff, created by Bud Fisher who was the actual owner of the studio. When Barre and Powers had a falling out several years later, Fisher took personal charge of the studio renaming it simply the Mutt and Jeff Studio.

Those early animated efforts featured the same conceits popular in comic strips. The characters talked in speech balloons. Beads of sweat literally popped off characters' heads when they were nervous or scared. Thin black lines indicated speed or impact with the ground. The first book to cover the art of animation, Edward Lutz's *Animated Cartoons: How They Are Made, Their Origin and Development* (1920) formalized many of these conceits into actual rules that should be followed in producing animation.

As animation increased in popularity, newer studios found that the most popular newspaper strip characters were already the property of other studios or that the royalties were expensive.

These new studios began developing original characters and when these characters became successful, they sometimes became the inspiration for newspaper strips.

The first real Cartoon Superstar was Felix the Cat. Created by Otto Messmer in 1919 for the Pat Sullivan studio, Felix was a black cat who helped define the concept of personality animation. He became as popular as many live action film stars and his films were often wild flights of fancy. Fortunately, thanks to his cleverness and detachable body, he was usually victorious despite whatever challenges confronted him.

It was not surprising when King Features syndicate began syndicating a Felix the Cat Sunday page

on August 14, 1923. A daily strip began on May 9, 1927. (Actually, there was a daily Felix newspaper strip from King Features in the London Illustrated News as early as 1922.)

Both Sunday and daily versions were written and drawn by Felix's creator, Otto Messmer, but he was not allowed to sign the strip with his name until the 1940s. The daily strip lasted until January 1, 1967 while Messmer continued to work on it only until 1954, when he turned it over to Joe Oriolo. The Sunday strip ended on August 19, 1943. Oriolo is best known as the person who redesigned Felix and gave him his magic bag of tricks when he produced the well-remembered television show in 1958.

Messmer's newspaper strip work was reprinted in early comic books. (Messmer also did original stories of Felix for comic books as did Oriolo.) The comic strip benefited from Messmer's strong draftsmanship and understanding of the character. The strips were similar to the cartoons where anything might happen. The daily strips shifted between being gag-a-day and loosely story oriented.

The strips mirrored the logic of the animated cartoons. While exploring a mysterious island with a professor, the clever cat found he could use a huge spider not only as an umbrella frame covered with palm fronds but could stretch the spider's legs into forming a cage for capturing a rare bird.

Another Cartoon Superstar was Betty Boop who made her first screen appearance in 1930. It took two years for her appearance to transform into the image audiences recognize today. This sexy little teaser found her way onto the comic strip page July 23, 1934 in a daily and November 24, 1934 in a Sunday version drawn by Bud Counihan, reportedly an artist from the Max Fleischer studio. The daily strip lasted until March 23, 1935, while the Sunday version continued through 1937. King Features was the

Above:
The first Betty Boop daily comic strip from 1934. © King Features Syndicate.

syndicate.

Counihan was able to capture the spirit of Betty as she worked as a star in Hollywood and had to battle directors, agents and assorted other perils. The strip lacked the darker film noir tones of the animated cartoons and even the Hollywood setting didn't produce some of the insane, dreamlike adventures of the early Betty cartoons. Betty's pals, Bimbo and Ko-Ko, were inexplicably absent.

Concerned citizens became outraged by the supposedly low moral behavior in films and not even cartoon characters like Betty Boop could escape these crusaders. As the animated cartoon toned down Betty's sexual appeal, so did the comic strip. The spotlight shifted to Betty's Aunt Tille and her small friend, Hunky Dory. The strip was canceled almost a year before Fleischer stopped making Betty Boop animated shorts.

In the mid-Eighties, Betty Boop and Felix were combined in a new strip from King Feature entitled *Betty Boop and Felix.* Four of the sons of Mort (*Beetle Bailey*) Walker - Greg, Brian, Morgan and Neal-collaborated on the short lived strip that started November 19, 1984 as a daily and Sunday.

The strip featured the classic Betty Boop costume, including the famous garter. The pair lived in a spacious and expensive New York apartment. The strip was a gag-a-day style that revolved around Betty working as an actress and model. Felix, for the most part, never talked but communicated through thought balloons. He was more than Betty's pet; he had a life of his own. While Betty associated with the beautiful

Below:
Betty Boop and Felix in the '80s.
© King Features Syndicate

January 13, 1930 saw the introduction of the daily Mickey Mouse comic strip from King Features. Those early strips were written by Walt Disney, himself, up until May 17, 1930.

Most papers headed the strip as "Mickey Mouse by Iwerks" with Walt Disney's famous signature not appearing until March 11, 1930, at the bottom of the last panel. The reason for this odd heading was that the strip was drawn by Ub Iwerks. Iwerks had quite literally drawn the first few Mickey Mouse animated cartoons by himself and was the natural choice to transfer Mickey's antics to the newspaper page. After the 18th strip, Iwerks left and his

Features, Mickey's adventures became story continuities on April 1, 1930. Gottfredson took over the writing after Walt left and was responsible for a series of continuity stories that have rarely been surpassed. He plotted stories with a variety of writers on the strip including Webb Smith, Ted Osborne, Merrill de Maris, Dick Shaw and Bill Walsh.

A Mickey Sunday page began January 10, 1932. Until 1938, Gottfredson was the artist when he turned it over to others like Manuel Gonzales and Bill Wright.

In the strip, Mickey Mouse was an adventurous hero battling bandits, pirates, crooks and mad scientists. Unfortunately, over the

people, Felix partied with his back alley pals.

By the start of 1930, Mickey Mouse had already appeared in 15 animated adventures (with nine more scheduled for that year). Inspired by that popularity,

inker, Win Smith, continued drawing the gag-a-day format until he was replaced on May 5, 1930, by Floyd Gottfredson, who would end up drawing the strip for several decades.

At the request of King

years, this image no longer matched the corporate image of Mickey and with the change in newspaper readership. King Features requested the strip be changed to a gag-a-day format and it continued in that format until it ceased production in 1989.

Almost immediately, the strip was revamped and in 1990 it reappeared. These strips shifted between daily gags and short story continuities. One of the major contributors to the "new look" is writer and artist Jim Engel, whose distinctive artwork graces greeting cards, cartoon stickers and promotional items. Disney still oversees production of the strip. For example Disney writer Floyd Norman acts as an in-house story editor. Reportedly, since the change in the strip, it has shown an increase in circulation.

Disney has had close to a dozen different newspaper strips over the years. Silly Symphonies was a Sunday color page begun on January 10, 1932, that featured serialized adaptations of Disney cartoons. For the first decade, it was written primarily by Ted Osborne, Merrill de Maris and Hubie Karp with Al Taliaferro supplying the art for stories like "The Adventures of Elmer Elephant," "Peculiar Penguins," "The Practical Pig" and "The Three Little Kittens." When Taliaferro left to take over the Donald Duck strip, other artists were Bob Grant, Hank Porter, Paul Murry and Dick Moores. They did adaptations of some of the Disney features like *Snow White*, *Pinocchio*, *Bambi* and *Cinderella*.

By the late Thirties, Donald Duck's popularity had eclipsed Mickey Mouse's fame so King Features felt a Donald Duck strip would be a big seller. Donald's daily strip began February 7, 1938, and a Sunday version began December 10, 1939. For many years, these strips were written by Bob Karp and drawn by Al Taliaferro. Supposedly, it was Karp and Taliaferro who were responsible for the creation of some key Disney characters like Huey, Dewey and Louie and Grandma Duck. The strips were harmless gag-a-day situations, although that did not prevent the strip from being criticized by Bolivia who felt the use of a comical St. Bernard named Bolivar in the strip was making fun of their country's greatest national hero, Simon Bolivar.

When Taliaferro died in 1969, the artwork was taken over by Frank Grundeen, who had worked as an animator at Disney since 1936. By the Eighties, the Donald Duck strip was being done by Bob Foster and Frank Smith. At the end of 1989, Disney ceased production of the strip, but King Features hired a new staff of freelancers and continues the gag-a-day feature under the same guidance as the new Mickey Mouse strip.

Disney's *Song Of The South* feature led to the Uncle Remus Sunday page which started October 14, 1945. It was drawn at various times by Paul Murry, Dick Moores, Riley Thompson, Bill Wright, Chuck Fuson, Mike Arens and John Ushler. The writing of these new adventures of B'rer Rabbit, B'rer Fox and B'rer Bear, which officially ended December 31, 1972, was primarily the work of George Stallings with the last decade being written by Jack Boyd.

An "original" Disney strip was Merry Menagerie, a daily black and white panel with talking animals. It ran from January 13, 1947 to March 17, 1962 and was written by Bob Karp and drawn by Bob Grant. The Treasury of Classic Tales began in 1952 and was written by Frank Reilly and drawn by John Ushler. It, like the Silly Symphony strip featured comic adaptations of various Disney features and TV shows. It continued into the Eighties with various artists, including Jack Kirby and Mike Royer who produced an adaptation of Disney's *The Black Hole*. Disney's live action animal series inspired a True Life Adventures strip beginning in 1955 written by Dick Huemer and drawn by George Wheeler. It only lasted a few years.

The successful *Lady And The Tramp* (1955) was spun-off into the ever popular Scamp. Scamp, which began in 1955, was the mischievous gray offspring of Lady and Tramp. He also had a successful run in comic books illustrated by Al Hubbard.

The comic strip, which was a gag-a-day strip, was originally written by Bill Berg. Artists over the years who reportedly contributed to the daily were Manuel Gonzales, Mike Arens, Dick Moores, Roger Armstrong and John Ushler. The strip ceased in 1988.

It took over two decades for Disney to introduce its next strip. *Winnie the Pooh* debuted in 1978 and ran until 1988. It was more closely tied to the animated shorts than A.A. Milne's famous books. However, Disney's crew (which included Don Ferguson writing and Sparky Moore drawing) did borrow a knight mentioned in the first Winnie the Pooh book, but never animated by Disney, and converted him to Sir Brian. They then created a

Opposite page: Wile E. Coyote has the spotlight in this Bugs Bunny Sunday strip from 1990. © 1990 Warner Brothers

Below: Disney's Peter Pan aides Santa Claus in a special Christmas story strip.© Walt Disney Productions

Dragon, who was an encyclopedia salesman, to work with the knight.

Within the last decade, Disney has tried to re-invade the newspaper page with the introduction of *Gummi Bears* in 1986. It was a one panel, gag-a-day strip based on the TV show. One gag featured the Gummi Bears freezing in a snow covered landscape while Zummi says, *"Dagnabit!* Tummi left his freezer door open again!"* Sundays, the strip would feature mazes, puzzles and other interactive activities.

The strip proved a short lived attempt to cash in on a mid-Eighties trend of aiming comic strips at a younger audience. The trend died when it was determined that children only read the color Sunday comic sections. Like all Disney efforts, it was professionally done even though it sparked little general interest at the time, finally exiting in 1988. Writers included Don

Dougherty and later Lee Nordling with art chores generally by Rick Hoover.

There were many special strips created for limited runs around the Christmas season. These strips were generally based on Disney characters or films but had a Christmas theme. One had Peter Pan helping Santa Claus retrieve stolen presents from Captain Hook and his pirates.

Indirectly, Disney contributed greatly to newspaper strips. Many Disney artists left the studio in the Forties and found even more success as creators of popular comic strips.

Some of the Disney artists who went on to comic strip fame include Hank Ketcham (Dennis the Menace), George Baker (Sad Sack), Virgil "VIP" Partch (Big George and others), and Walt Kelly (Pogo).

Other Disney artists weren't always as fortunate. Dick Huemer, a Disney

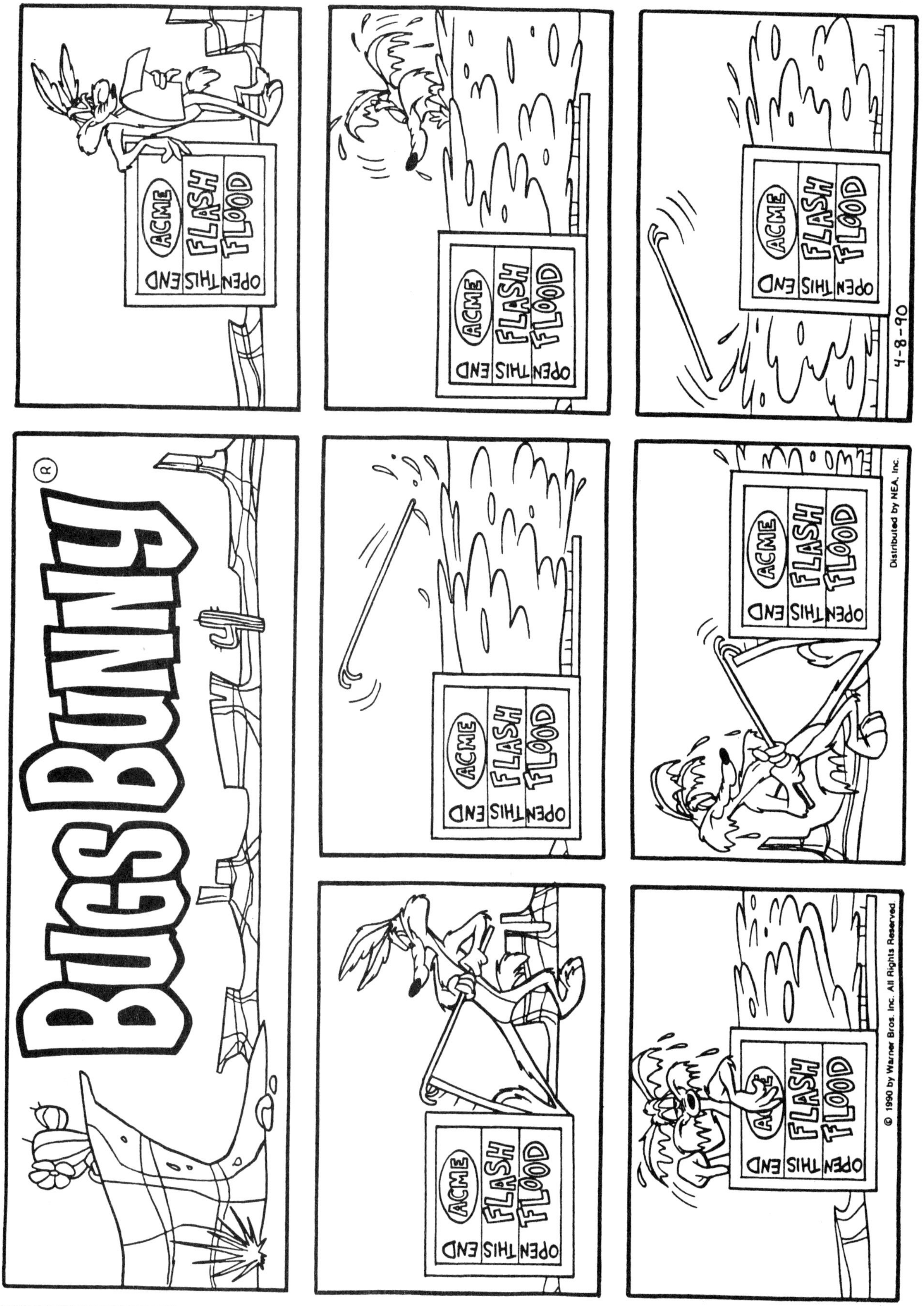
BUGS BUNNY
ACME
FLASH FLOOD
OPEN THIS END
ACME
FLASH FLOOD
OPEN THIS END
ACME
FLASH FLOOD
OPEN THIS END
ACME
FLASH FLOOD
OPEN THIS END
ACME
FLASH FLOOD
OPEN THIS END
ACME
FLASH FLOOD
OPEN THIS END
ACME
FLASH FLOOD
OPEN THIS END
4-8-90
© 1990 by Warner Bros. Inc. All Rights Reserved
Distributed by NEA, Inc.

storyman for such films as *Dumbo*, and Paul Murry, famous for his work on Mickey Mouse comic books, tried to do a humorous cowboy strip, Buck O'Rue, that lasted from January 15, 1951 to 1953.

Disney alumni were not the only animation artists to attempt syndication via the newspaper. Van Boring was a strip from the Thirties by "Tish Tash," the nickname of director Frank Tashlin who was also directing Porky Pig cartoons at the time. (It was rumored that one of the reasons Tashlin left animation was that Leon Schlesinger wanted a cut

Above:
1954's Barker Bill by Paul Terry, owner of Terrytoons.
© McNaught Syndicate

Below:
Bullwinkle strip from the '60s.
© Pat-Ward Productions

from the money that Tashlin was getting for his strip about a large, roly-poly man because Tashlin might have been working on it on company time.) Myron Waldman, a head animator at Fleischer's, did Happy the Humbug for the Post Hall Syndicate.

Chuck Jones was responsible for a short lived strip entitled Crawford (1977) about an imaginative young boy. Another strip about a young boy was Terr'ble Thompson by Gene Deitch, the director responsible for some of the Sixties *Popeye* cartoons, some unusual MGM *Tom and Jerrys*

and *Tom Terrific. Barker Bill* was a strip from 1954-'55 credited to Paul Terry. Obviously, Terry by this time was not directly involved with this comic strip but, like Walt Disney, his name value would hopefully attract readers. Tom Morrison, a Terrytoons storyman and the voice of Mighty Mouse, scripted the circus oriented strip.

While it may seem that Disney inspired strips tried to dominate the comic strip page, other animation studios had little trouble launching strips. Bugs Bunny got his own Sunday strip from NEA in 1942

originally done by Chase Craig. By 1948 a daily version was begun, written by Jack Taylor and drawn by Ralph Heimdahl. Heimdahl is the artist most closely associated with the strip over its many decades. He eventually took over work on the Sunday strip.

The writer for both strips during this long association was Al Stoffel. When asked about his accomplishment on the strip, Stoffel replied, "I'm proudest of my development of Sylvester. I think of him as a combination of Wimpy and W.C. Fields with the seat out his pants...Although I've seen several hundred animated Bugs cartoons over the years, that work is quite different from ours. The animated cartoons depend mostly on action, sound and voice characterizations for their impact. In the strip we have to try to translate these characteristics into cartoons which don't move and the printed word which has no sound. It ain't easy."

Among other writers and artists involved at various times with the strip were Carl Fallberg, Roger Armstrong and Tom McKimson. The strip featured not only Bugs but the whole Looney Tunes crew at various times. However, by the Seventies, the strip had comfortably settled in to a very domesticated atmosphere reminiscent of some of the comic book stories. It was a

situation comedy world where formerly raucous characters lived in houses, went to conservative jobs, worked in stores and exhibited none of the wacky animal inspired humor of the shorts.

With the resurgence of interest in Warners' characters during the late Eighties, the strip was radically revamped under the direction of Kathleen Helppie and Darrel Van Citters to more closely reproduce the early Warners humor of wild gags, puns and crazy situations. The writing for the strip was handled by John Cawley and Brett Koth with ex-Disney animator Shawn Keller doing the art. This new version sadly received limited distribution and was canceled on December 31, 1990.

Saperstein Productions packaged a Mr. Magoo strip for the Chicago Tribune Syndicate during the mid-Sixties. Pete Alvarado is credited as being the artist who brought the adventures of the near sighted old man to life for newspapers. The strip was closely inspired by UPA's Sixties television cartoons with Waldo and Charlie the houseboy making frequent appearances as foils for Magoo's blind humor. The strip was popular enough to be collected in three paperback books beginning with *The Nearsighted Mister*

"IT'S OKAY, YOGI ---- HE'S ON A LEASH!"

*Above:
Yogi's panel from
1974.
© McNaught
Syndicate*

Magoo (Pyramid Books, 1967).

Jay Ward's characters were also popular during the Sixties. The prime time series *The Bullwinkle Show* which premiered in 1961 established Rocky the Flying Squirrel and Bullwinkle Moose as Cartoon Superstars after their syndicated appearances on *Rocky And His Friends*. Still, it probably surprised few folks to see the McClure Syndicate release a Bullwinkle strip. This short lived (1962-64) and very funny recreation of Ward's wildness was written and illustrated by Al Kilgore. The strip was a series of story continuities. In one, Boris and Natasha try to sabotage the "O-Bomb" project (remember, this was the time of "A-Bombs" and "H-Bombs"). Another had

Bullwinkle disrupting Madison Avenue by doing a series of "truthful" commercials.

However, the kings of animated television for many years were Hanna-Barbera and two of their legendary creations got their chance at newspaper fame. In 1961, McNaught Syndicate launched both a Yogi Bear

Above:
The Flintstones in 1974. © McNaught Syndicate

Below:
A sample of He-Man's short lived comic strip from 1987. © McNaught Syndicate

and a Flintstones comic strip. Harvey Eisenberg drew the Yogi Bear Sunday strips until 1965 when Gene Hazelton took over. There was also a gag-a-day daily which featured all the familiar Jellystone Park characters like Yogi, Boo Boo and Ranger Smith.

The Flintstones, the modern stone age family,

had both a Sunday and a daily strip. Once again Harvey Eisenberg (also known for his work on the Tom and Jerry comic book) did the first several Flintstone Sundays. For the first two years or so, Roger Armstrong illustrated Fred and the gang. The best known *Flintstones'* artist is Gene Hazelton who drew

the strip for decades. Once again, it was a gag-a-day format.

Unfortunately, many of the strips mentioned in this article were not available in all papers and some readers may be unfamiliar with them. Even more amazing are the many animation oriented strips that only a handful of collectors know existed. For instance, the Woody Woodpecker daily strip ran from 1954 to 1961 and was supervised by Al Stoffel. It has never been reprinted.

He-Man was a short lived strip by G. Forton and C. Weber that was distributed by the McNaught Syndicate in the mid-Eighties. It was based on the popular Filmation television series and its art style resembled superhero comic books of the period. There was both a daily and a Sunday with a continuing adventure story of the heroes of Eternia battling evil.

Some animation related strips were prepared for possible syndication, but never made it to newspapers. One was a pantomime strip starring the Pink Panther. The Don Bluth studio made an unsuccessful attempt to syndicate a comic panel based on their first production, *Banjo The Woodpile Cat*. The panel was done by Bluth animators Will Finn (writer) and Lorna Pomeroy (artist). Prior to the unsuccessful late Eighties

Saturday morning revival, Bob Clampett's *Beany And Cecil* were developed as a strip by Brett Koth (art) and John Cawley (writer) under the supervision of the Clampett family.

Today just as in the early days it is common for popular newspaper characters like Garfield, Cathy, Hagar, Marvin, B.C. and the Peanuts kids to be transferred to animation.

Above:
Proposed comic panel starring Don Bluth's Banjo character.
© 1982 Banjo Productions.

"I've always seen Garfield as an animated character in my mind," creator Jim Davis commented in an exclusive interview in Cartoon Quarterly, "Being forced to stop his action in three frames every day is much more difficult than letting him run wild for 24 minutes in an animated special."

As the Nineties begin, new animated stars are also hoping to continue the

Animated Stripping

tradition of finding additional fame as newspaper stars. There have been preliminary discussions to transfer the new Warners' *Tiny Toon Adventures'* stars and the irreverent *Simpsons* into their own comic strips.

Ironically, one of the big

Above:
Proposed Pink Panther comic strip created by MGM/UA in the mid-sixties.
© UAC-Geoffrey

animated projects that will hopefully appear in the Nineties is a feature film version of *Little Nemo* which has been in production for almost a decade. (A syndicated animated series based on the strip is set to debut in 1991.) Over 80 years

after Winsor McCay started the cross-over tradition between animated cartoons and newspaper strips, his characters will once again entertain audiences in theaters.

Above:
Proposed comic strip starring Bob Clampett's Beany and Cecil from the late '80s.
© Bob Clampett

TOP SECRET

CHAPTER FIFTEEN:

**THE ENVELOPE
P-P-P-PLEASE!
OSCAR WINNING
ANIMATION**

l try
into
l
oor,
e to

1al

will
w

lar
en

m

e

The Envelope P-p-p-please! Oscar Winning Animation

"That Oscar winning rabbit, Bugs Bunny!" is a phrase that sticks in the minds of most people. However, Bugs' one Oscar does not even make a dent in the list of nearly sixty animated Oscars handed out since 1932. Who are the other winners?

Unlike their live action counterparts, animated Oscars often go to films that few people have had the opportunity to see and many did not even know existed. At the Oscar ceremonies, some of Hollywood's top stars read off a list of three to five animated shorts nominated for the award of Best Short Subject, Animated. Even the presenters are often perplexed by the titles.

The classic example of this situation was when *The Fly* won the Oscar at the 1981 ceremonies. A man bounded up to the podium to accept the award. He later attended the Governor's Ball at the Beverly Hilton following the show and had the Oscar proudly displayed on his table. The next morning, the Academy had to recover the statue when it was learned that the mysterious man was not the winner. The Oscar was then shipped to the Hungarian director of *The Fly*, Ferenc Rofusc.

Such confusion is not surprising. For decades, the major U.S. studios have not produced animated shorts in any regular fashion. Since

Above: Walt Disney, here with an early award, won the first eight Oscars for animated short subjects. © Walt Disney Company

the Sixties, the majority of animated shorts have been produced in foreign countries, often under grants by the governments there. Others are student or experimental films. These shorts have not generally received any public screenings outside of animation festivals.

In the late Eighties this began to change slightly. The Walt Disney studio began producing a series of shorts starring their new celebrity Roger Rabbit. The success of these shorts spurred Warner Brothers to produce a new theatrical short starring their heavy hitters: Bugs Bunny, Daffy Duck and Elmer Fudd. Twentieth Century Fox announced they would also begin producing "Foxtoons"

for showing in front of selected features and Universal is gearing up for a new theatrical short starring their own Woody Woodpecker.

Oddly, the first Roger Rabbit short, *Tummy Trouble*, failed to be even nominated for an Oscar. Many of the artists on the short complained that the Academy of Motion Picture Arts and Sciences was purposefully ignoring U.S. animation in lieu of foreign product. Once again, animated fans and critics alike wondered "how do they pick the winner?"

The Oscar Process

The Academy of Motion Picture Arts and Sciences was the concept of the late Louis B. Mayer who decided there was a need for such an organization to give status and respect to the motion picture industry. With the help of other prominent figures in Hollywood, the Academy was created and its first, then nameless, statuettes were presented at a banquet on May 16, 1929.

The Short Subject Awards were first handed out in 1932 in three separate categories: Cartoon, Comedy and Novelty. Today, the Short Subjects Awards are broken down into two categories: live-action and animation.

The Academy defines an animated film as usually falling into one of two general fields of animation:

character or abstract. Some of the techniques for animating films recognized by the Academy include cel animation, computer animation, stop-motion animation, clay animation, puppets, pixilation, cutouts, pins, camera multiple pass imagery, kaleidoscopic effects and drawing on the film frame, itself.

Short animated films may not be more than thirty minutes in running time. Dialogue or narration must be substantially in English or the film must have English subtitles.

How does a film get to finally qualify and get nominated? According to a 1987 Academy handbook, to qualify for the 1987 Oscar (*The Man Who Planted Trees* won), an animated film had to fulfill one of the following criteria:

(1) It must have had its first original exhibition within two years of completion date in a commercial motion picture theater in Los Angeles County for a paid full theatrical release of three consecutive days (no fewer than two screenings per day) between December 1, 1986 and November 30, 1987.

(2) Or it must have participated in a "recognized" competitive film festival within two years of completion dated between December 1, 1986 and November 30, 1987 prior to any other public exhibition

and must have won a best-in-category award.

(3) or finally, an animated short would be eligible for award consideration within two years of completion date if it had been recognized by the Council on Non-theatrical Events (CINE) in the form of a Golden Eagle Award. (According to the Academy handbook, the final winning entries in the Academy's Annual Student Film Awards competition for 1987 would also be eligible.)

Television specials are submitted ("Television exhibition in the Los Angeles area does not disqualify a film, provided such exhibition occurs after its Los Angeles theatrical release.") However, TV specials rarely get past the preliminaries. The sole exception was Richard Williams' *A Christmas Carol* which won an Oscar in 1972.

Once eligibility has been established, a Reviewing Committee views all films and marks each entry 10 (excellent), 8 (good), 6 (fair) or 4 (poor). Not more than ten nor fewer than six films receiving the highest average scores above 7.5 are considered further.

The entries selected by the Reviewing Committee are then screened by the Branch Nominating Committee, consisting of all active members of the Academy Short Films Branch. The point system is

the same as the Reviewing Committee. Those films receiving an average score of 8.0 or more become the nominations. (There may be not more than five nor fewer than three nominations in this category.)

Final voting for the Short Films Awards is restricted to active and life Academy members who may vote only at a special Academy screening of the nominated achievements. (Members of the Short Films Branch who served on the Nominating Committee and who viewed all the nominated films can receive ballots by mail.)

According to the Academy Handbook, "Excellence of the entries shall be judged on the basis of originality, entertainment and production quality without regard to cost of production or subject

*Below:
Walter Lantz, in this publicity still from the '60s, won an honorary Oscar in 1979 for the creation of Woody Woodpecker.
© Walter Lantz*

Above: Tom and Jerry, the most Oscar-honored cartoon characters, in Cat Concerto. © MGM

matter."

The preliminary screenings are held in December and January and one past member of the committee has described the screening of the animated shorts by mentioning that members view each short for five minutes. If the short is longer than five minutes, the members signal by a show of hands or flashlights whether they want to continue viewing the film or turn it off.

After a cartoon gets past the first screening, it is shown to the general membership in a nomination screening usually held in February. Many times, the general membership has different preferences than the preliminary committee and a "dark horse" gets into the fray.

If two shorts that seem equally strong are nominated, sometimes a third nominee that didn't seem to have much of a chance will go on to win. According to one past member, that was the case in 1976 (*Leisure*) and 1986 (*A Greek Tragedy*).

Keeping Score

Physically, an Oscar is

ten inches tall, weighs about seven pounds and is fashioned of gold plate over bronze. It has been estimated that cost of each statuette is about two hundred dollars. For the winners of the statue, though, its real value is priceless. (Winners must sign a form stating that they will sell the statue back to the Academy should they ever not wish to keep it. Despite this, in the late Eighties some Oscars began to show up at auction houses where they fetched thousands of dollars from eager bidders.)

While many movie fans can rattle off a list of the most (Oscar) honored stars and directors, few animation collectors can do the same when it comes to the animated winners. Everyone is aware that the Disney studio has won the most, but after that there is little immediate memory.

Over the years, the studios which have won the most statuettes have been led by Disney with thirteen. Coming in second was MGM with nine (seven of which were Tom and Jerry shorts). In third is Warner Brothers with five. Tied in fourth place is UPA, Storyboard Films and the National Film Board of Canada with three each.

In the area of directors, topping the list of the most honored directors are Bill Hanna and Joe Barbera with seven, all for their MGM Tom and Jerry shorts.

Warner Brothers' Friz Freleng is second with five (one was when he was at DePatieFreleng). John Hubley won three at his Storyboard Films. Finally there are those who have won two Oscars each: Frederick Back (at the National Film Board of Canada), Pete Burness (at UPA), Burt Gillette (at Disney), David Hand (at Disney), Wilfred Jackson (at Disney), Chuck Jones (one at Warners, one at MGM), and Ward Kimball (at Disney).

The top winning Cartoon Superstars are Tom and Jerry. The famed cat and mouse team won seven Oscars, more than any living actor. Those coming closest to this team are the stars who have won two Oscars each: Mister Magoo (UPA) and Tweety and Sylvester (Warner Brothers). Animated actors winning a single Oscar are Bugs Bunny, Gerald McBoing Boing, Pepe LePew, the Pink Panther, Pluto (with co-star Mickey Mouse), and Speedy Gonzales (Sylvester the Cat co-stars).

Special Oscars have been given to Walt Disney twice. Once in 1931 "for the creation of Mickey Mouse" and again in 1938 for *Snow White And The Seven Dwarfs* (this was an "altered" statue and featured one large Oscar and seven little Oscars). Others receiving special Oscars are Walter Lantz in 1979 for creating Woody

Woodpecker and Richard Williams in 1989 for the creation of Roger Rabbit.

The Winners

Following is a listing of animated shorts winning the Oscar for Best Animated Short. Many of the major studio releases are now available on home video through their respective owners. *The Whole Toon Catalog* (Post Office Box 369, Issaquah, Washington 98027) offers many of these collections. Some of the more recent independent and foreign films are also receiving distribution on

Below: Original theatrical poster of The Two Mousketeers, Tom and Jerry's *sixth Oscar winner.* © *MGM*

Above:
The last Silly
Symphony
produced.
© Walt Disney
Productions

home video. Expanded Entertainment (Post Office Box 25547, Los Angeles, California 90025) offers some of these. Write both for recent catalogs.

Key to the following list is **'Year-Title** (studio/director) synopsis.

1931/1932 - *Flowers And Trees* (Disney/Burt Gillett)

The love between two trees is put to the ultimate test when a jealous rival starts a forest fire. The first animated film in Three-Strip Technicolor.

1932/1933 - *Three Little Pigs*
(Disney/Burt Gillett)

One of the most famous cartoons in animation history tells the story of the three pigs building houses to protect themselves from a big, bad wolf. The song ("Who's Afraid of the Big Bad Wolf") became a national hit and Disney later followed up the short with three sequels: *The Big Bad Wolf* (1934), *The Three Little Wolves* (1936), and *The Practical Pig* (1939).

1934 - *The Tortoise And The Hare* (Disney/Wilfred Jackson)

Based on the classic Aesop fable that teaches the moral that slow and steady sometimes wins the race. Max Hare is erroneously credited as being a predecessor to Bugs Bunny. Max and the tortoise (Toby) reappeared in *Toby Tortoise Returns* (1936).

1935 - *Three Orphan Kittens* (Disney/David Hand)

Three abandoned kittens cause havoc in a house but are saved from being tossed back into the snow by the little girl of the house. One of Disney's early experiments with adding dimension. The studio tried painting some of the backgrounds on cels so perspective could be utilized a bit more. A similar process (done with computers) is utilized today.

1936 - *Country Cousin* (Disney/David Hand)

A country mouse (Abner) visits his cousin (Monty) in the big city and has a night out on the town that leads to his later distress.

1937 - *The Old Mill* (Disney/Wilfred Jackson)

An old mill and its animal inhabitants weather a violent storm. This is the first film to utilize the Multiplane camera. This giant camera provided additional dimension by allowing overlays and underlays to be painted on levels of glass. These glass levels could be moved independently of cels and the background creating an illusion of dimension and depth.

1938 - *Ferdinand The Bull* (Disney/Dick Rickard)

Based on the book by Munro Leaf and Robert Lawson, the story recounts the adventures of a bull who would rather smell flowers than fight. It is reported that Disney provided the voice of Ferdinand's mother and caricatures of Disney animators and Disney, himself, appear in the bullfighting arena

1939 - *The Ugly Duckling* (Disney/Jack Cutting)

Hans Christian Anderson's tale of an outcast duckling who later discovers he is a swan. A remake of the 1931 Disney black-and-white version. This was the last *Silly Symphony* produced. Disney replaced the series

with occasional "Specials."
1940 - *The Milky Way* (MGM/Rudolph Ising)

Three little kittens, who lost their mittens, are sent to bed without dinner. There they dream of visiting the Milky Way in a balloon basket so they can satisfy their hunger.

1941 - *Lend A Paw* (Disney/ Clyde Geronimi)

Pluto becomes jealous when a stray kitten seemingly steals Mickey Mouse's affection. A remake of the black-and-white *Mickey's Pal Pluto* (1933). This is Mickey's only appearance in an Oscar winning short.

1942 - *Der Fuehrer's Face* (Disney/Jack Kinney)

Donald Duck dreams he's in "Naziland" (the original title for this short) and doesn't like it. When he cracks under the pressure, the imagery runs wild and is reminiscent of the "Pink Elephant" sequence from *Dumbo* (1941). Source of the popular Spike Jones song that boosted spirits in World War II.

1943 - *Yankee Doodle Mouse* (MGM/Bill Hanna and Joe Barbera)

With an assortment of toys and fireworks, Tom and Jerry engage in combat in the basement of a house. Jerry repeatedly sends military style communiques to an unknown party. The last

reads "Send more cats. Signed, Lieutenant Jerry Mouse."

1944 - *Mouse Trouble* (MGM/ Bill Hanna and Joe Barbera)

Tom receives a book on "How to Catch a Mouse" (from Random Mouse) and proceeds to go after Jerry with everything from stethoscopes to shotguns to a mechanical mouse. Tom only succeeds in blowing up the house.

1945 - *Quiet Please* (MGM/ Bill Hanna and Joe Barbera)

After disturbing Spike the bulldog's rest, Tom tries to keep it quiet, but Jerry is determined to awaken the dog trying everything from dropping light bulbs to dynamite. Tom continually suffers Spike's fury.

1946 - *The Cat Concerto* (MGM/Bill Hanna and Joe Barbera)

Tom tries to play the piano at a fancy concert hall but is continually interrupted by Jerry who makes his home in the keyboard. (Most books list this film as being released in 1947, and it is copyright 1947.) Similar to Warner Brothers' *Rhapsody Rabbit* (1946), in which Bugs Bunny tries to play the piano and is distracted by a mouse.

1947 - *Tweetie Pie* (Warner Brothers/Friz Freleng)

Tweetie the canary is taken out of the cold and

into the house much to the disgust of "Thomas" (Sylvester) the housecat who tries to get the bird. Warner Brothers' first Oscar winning cartoon and the first teaming of Tweetie and Sylvester.

1948 - *The Little Orphan* (MGM/Bill Hanna and Joe Barbera)

Jerry tries to care for a little orphan mouse named Nibbles (sometimes referred to as Tuffy in comic books) who insists on drinking milk from Tom's bowl. When Tom spanks Nibbles, Jerry goes wild and beats Tom to a pulp.

*Below:
Poster for 1950's winner.
© UPA*

165

1949 - *For Scent-Imental Reasons* (Warner Brothers/Chuck Jones)

Pepe LePew's adventures in a perfume shop. The shop keeper tosses in a cat (who gets the traditional white stripe painted on her) and the chase is on until Pepe is painted blue. Suddenly he becomes the hunted once the paint covers his smell.

1950 - *Gerald McBoing Boing* (UPA/Robert Cannon)

Based on the children's record by Dr. Seuss about a boy who only talks in sound effects and the problems this situation creates for him and his family.

1951 - *The Two Mouseketeers* (MGM/Bill Hanna and Joe Barbera)

Set in the France of Dumas' *Three Musketeers*, Tom, in a guard's costume, must protect a large dinner from the sword wielding "mouseketeers," Jerry and Nibbles. Nibbles speaks some French and by the end Tom gets the guillotine. (Most books list this film as being released in 1952 and it is copyright 1952.) This setup became the basis for numerous comic stories and three animated sequels, *Touche Pussy Cat* (1954), *Tom And Cherie* (1955) and *Royal Catnap* (1958).

1952 - *Johann Mouse* (MGM/Bill Hanna and Joe Barbera)

Jerry is Johann Mouse who lives in the home of

Johann Strauss. He can't resist dancing to a Strauss waltz even when Tom is the one playing the piano. When the staff discovers Tom's ability he and Jerry become performers.

1953 - *Toot, Whistle, Plunk And Boom* (Disney/Charles Nichols and Ward Kimball)

Disney's first cartoon in Cinemascope traces the history of music back to four essential sounds. A sequel to *Melody* (1953) and done in a stylized, limited animation approach similar to UPA. One of the "Adventures in Music" shorts, hosted by Professor Owl.

*Below:
Two time winner
Mr. Magoo.
© UPA*

1954 - *When Magoo Flew* (UPA/Pete Burness)

Mr. Magoo boards a big jet thinking it is a movie theater and finds himself in a real life adventure with an escaped thief involving some suspensful wing walking. At the end, Magoo comments that he enjoyed the "movie" but regrets the "theater" didn't also show a cartoon.

1955 - *Speedy Gonzales* (Warner Brothers/Friz Freleng)

Speedy, the fastest mouse in all of Mexico, helps his friends raid a cheese factory guarded by Sylvester the cat.

1956 - *Mr. Magoo's Puddle Jumper* (UPA/Pete Burness)

Magoo buys a Baker Electric car for his nephew Waldo but drives it off a pier and under the ocean with a motorcycle policeman in hot pursuit.

1957 - *Birds Anonymous* (Warner Brothers/Friz Freleng)

Trying to keep his home, Sylvester joins Birds Anonymous (B.A.) in an attempt to avoid eating Tweety. To help, a comrade from B.A. joins Sylvester at home, but soon the comrade has a bigger bird addiction problem than Sylvester.

1958 - *Knighty-Knight, Bugs* (Warner Brothers/Friz Freleng)

Bugs Bunny, the court

REMEMBER ME? FIRST I WAS A MOVIE TITLE... NOW I'M A MOVIE STAR!!!

He's back on the screen in his new, hilarious, very own Cartoon Series!

MIRISCH FILMS presents
BLAKE EDWARDS

THE PINK PANTHER

in

"THE PINK PHINK"

A Pink Panther Cartoon in COLOR

Produced by
DEPATIE-FRELENG ENTERPRISES
Pink Panther Theme by Henry Mancini

Released thru
UNITED ARTISTS

to win an Oscar shows a strange little man who creates his day at the beach by blowing up balloons that resemble the ocean, his girlfriend and a rival for her affections.

1962 - *The Hole* (Storyboard/ John Hubley)
Two construction workers, White and Black, converse about atomic annihilation when a crane accident convinces one that the bomb has already gone off.

1963 - *The Critic* (Pintoff-Crossbow/Ernest Pintoff)
Mel Brooks provides the voice of an unseen man in the audience of this abstract cartoon, mostly made up of cutout images. "Vot's dot? Is dat doity? Doit and filt."

1964 - *The Pink Phink* (United Artists-Depatie-Freleng/Friz Freleng)
The Panther tries to paint a house pink while the owner tries unsuccessfully to paint the same house blue. The first in the series of shorts based on the character introduced in the credit sequence of *The Pink Panther* (1964).

1965 - *The Dot And The Line* (MGM/Chuck Jones)
Based on the Norton Juster story of a dot who loves an unkempt squiggle. A determined line wins the dot's love by proving itself more versatile.

jester, battles the Black Knight (Yosemite Sam) and a fire-breathing dragon with hay fever. Bugs gets the Singing Sword and Sam gets blown to the Moon.

1959 - *Moonbird* (Storyboard/ John Hubley)
Two little boys set out to trap an ostrich which they think is a "moonbird."

1960 - *Munro* (Rembrandt/ Gene Deitch)
Story by Jules Feiffer about a four year old boy named Munro who is drafted into the U.S. Army but the Army refuses to admit the mistake.

1961 - *Ersatz* (Zagreb/Dusan Vukotic)
The first foreign cartoon

Above: From movie title to Oscar winner. © UAC-Geoffrey

The Envelope P-p-p-please! Oscar Winning Animation

1966 - *Herb Albert And The Tijuana Brass Double Feature* (Storyboard/John Hubley)

Two Herb Albert songs, "Tijuana Taxi" and "Spanish Flea," provide the Mexican themed storylines.

1967 - *The Box* (Murakami-Wolf/Fred Wolf)

A man walks into a bar with a box containing a blurred creature. A woman also walks in with another box containing another blurred creature. After the creatures fight to the death, the man and woman walk off.

1968 - *Winnie The Pooh And The Blustery Day* (Disney/Woolie Reitherman)

Pooh and his friends weather a violent storm. Tigger is introduced in this second featurette based on A. A. Milne's famous bear. Includes the surreal musical dream sequence "Heffalumps and Woozles" based heavily on "Pink Elephants" from *Dumbo* (1941). The short was later incorporated into the feature *The Many Adventures Of Winnie The Pooh* (1977).

1969 - *It's Tough To Be A Bird* (Disney/Ward Kimball)

A humorous look at birds and their problems coping with man. It features standard Disney animation plus animated cutouts and live action sequences. Later expanded into an episode of the Disney TV series.

1970 - *Is It Always Right To Be Right* (Bosustow Productions/Lee Mishkin)

A plea for moderation politics, told as an elaborate parable disguised as a slide film.

Below:
The star of 1984's Charade.
© *Michael Mills Production*

1971 - *The Crunch Bird* (Crunchbird Productions/Ted Petok)

The old bar joke about a

wife who likes unusual pets and buys a bird who attacks and "crunches" whatever it is told (like "Crunch Bird the chair") and who takes his final command too literally.

1972 - *A Christmas Carol*

(American Broadcasting Company Film Services/Richard Williams)

Alistair Sim, who portrayed Scrooge in an earlier live action film version, provides the voice for this retelling of Dickens' classic story, animated in the graphic black and white style of the 1890's. The first television cartoon to win an Oscar. Produced by Chuck Jones.

1973 - *Frank Film* (Frank Mouris Productions/Frank Mouris)

A collection of images and a double sound track that tells the life story of the filmmaker in seven minutes.

1974 - *Closed Mondays* (Lighthouse Productions/Will Vinton and Bob Guardiner)

One of Will Vinton's earliest Claymation shorts shows what happens when a drunken old man gets locked in a museum at night and the artwork comes to life.

1975 - *Great* (Grantstern Limited-British Lion Films/Bob Godfrey)

A half hour history of Pauval, inventor and designer of Leviathan, a gigantic steamship of the Victorian era.

1976 - *Leisure* (Film Australia/Suzanne Baker)

A fourteen minute lecture about the growth of man's leisure time in the machine age, illustrated with crude collage and cutout animation.

1977 - *Sand Castle* (National Film Board of Canada/Co Hoedman)

In a combination of sand and clay animation, a group of creatures emerge from the sand and pitch in to build an elaborate sand castle.

1978 - *Special Delivery* (National Film Board of Canada/John Weldon and Eunice Macauley)

The story of the circumstances surrounding the strange death of a Canadian postman.

1979 - *Every Child* (National Film Board of Canada/ Eugene Fedorenko)

An abandoned child is taken in only to be re-abandoned on a neighbor's door time after time.

1980 - *The Fly* (Panonia Films/Rofusz)

A remarkable journey into a house seen through a fly's eyes.

1981 - *Crac* (Societe Radio Canada/Frederick Back)

The story of a chair and the changes it witnesses in the Quebec village where she was made. She eventually finds a home in a museum.

1982 - *Tango* (Film Polski/ Zbigniew Rybczynski)

A special effects film in which a group of live-action characters are optically printed over a painted background of a kitchen. In the kitchen, actions are continually added and repeated, all in rhthym to a tango, until the cycles combine into a fascinating, visual treat.

1983 - *Sundae In New York* (Pickermation/Jimmy Picker)

Clay animation brings new life to the song "New York, New York" when a clay caricature of former New York Mayor Ed Koch sings the song and meets numerous celebrities also caricatured in clay.

1984 - *Charade* (Michael Mills Productions/Jon Minnis)

A contest in charades between two men. One does simple pantomime to illustrate complex ideas and succeeds while the other does elaborate pantomimes to illustrate simple ideas and fails. This independent production was made at Sheridan College and later reshot at Michael Mills Productions.

1985 - *Anna And Bella* (Netherland-Independent/ Borge Ring)

Two sisters reminisce about their girlhoods, especially their rivalry over a man.

**1986 - *A Greek Tragedy* (CineTe Puba/Nicole Van

Above:
Sisters Anna and Bella.
© Borge Ring

Goethen)

Three partially-toga-clad Greek women try to keep the Parthenon from collapsing, but it crumbles to pieces anyway.

1987 - *The Man Who Planted Trees* (Societe Radio Canada/ Frederic Back)

A man who lives in a desolate wilderness area continues to plant acorns in the ground over the years even though wars rage. Eventually his work is rewarded and the barren land is transformed.

1988 - *Tin Toy* (Pixar/John Lasseter)

A rather demonic baby pursues a little wind-up toy man who is a one man band that is attempting, with mixed results, to entertain the child. The first computer animated film to win an Oscar. The short is reminiscent of Lasseter's 1980 student film *Lady And The Lamp*.

1989 - *Balance* (Lauenstein Film Production/Wolfgang & Cristoph Lauenstein)

Stop motion short with puppets about four men on a platform out in space that remains balanced only so long as they stay at their respective corners on the platform. A mysterious box lands in the center and their desire to get the box upsets the balance.

1990 - *Creature Comforts* (Aardman Animations/Nick Park)

An amusing clay animation pseudo-documentary about a roving reporter interviewing animals in a London zoo. The dialog track was made by actual people in England discussing their lives and Park put those words into the mouths of a clay jaguar, turtle and other creatures.

Animated Presenters

In 1979, at the 51st Academy Awards, comedian Robin Williams presented Walter Lantz with an honorary Oscar. As an added treat, an animated Woody Woodpecker appeared on the TV screen as well to share the honor and thank Lantz.

An animated Bugs Bunny made two appearances at the Oscars to help present the Academy Award for the Best Animated Short. Bugs popped up in 1987 and 1990. In his 1990 presentation, he starred in a new animated sequence where he explained animation.

In 1989, while animated Disney characters watched from audience seats, an animated Mickey Mouse was on stage helping actor Tom Selleck present the Oscar for Best Animated Short.

At the 1991 Oscar ceremony, Woody Woodpecker, helped present the award. Like previous animated presenters, there were mutliple versions of Woody announcing the winner since there were three nominees in the category that year. Price Waterhouse informed the show's director Jeff Margulies of the winner about five minutes before Woody opened the animated envelope so that the right name could be read. Price Waterhouse has bent its vow of silence before for animated presenters and judging by the positive audience reaction to such events, it will have to do so again in the future.

Below:
That Oscar winning rabbit, Bugs Bunny, gest special award in What's Cookin' Doc *(1944).*
© *Warner Brothers*